Few investments in your children can return greater lifetime and eternal rewards than teaching them to manage money God's way. My friend Matt Bell has provided us with a helpful guide to accomplish just that.

CHUCK BENTLEY
CEO of Crown Financial Ministries and host of *My MoneyLife*

Helping young children get on a solid, God-glorifying financial path is a wonderful gift. It will help keep them from the financial challenges and pain so many adults experience. If you have children or grandchildren, *Trusted* is a great read. I heartily recommend it!

HOWARD DAYTON
Founder of Compass - finances God's way and author of *Your Money Counts*

Matt Bell's guide for teaching children how to manage money for a lifetime is a gem! Children crave their parents' trust, especially regarding money. Let Matt's experience and wisdom presented in *Trusted* take a big, scary topic and break it down into simple steps any family in any income bracket can follow. Building God-honoring trustworthiness in your children is an investment any parent can afford, one that is guaranteed to return huge dividends both now and for eternity.

MARY HUNT
Author of several personal finance books, including *Raising Financially Confident Kids*, and author of the *Everyday Cheapskate* syndicated column and blog

T0017727

In *Trusted*, Matt accomplishes the rare feat of faithfully teaching God's Word on the subject of money *and* applying that wisdom to modern-day financial life in a compelling way. Chock-full of practical advice and real-life examples, *Trusted* leaves readers well equipped to prepare our children to be wise financial stewards and ensure that we, the parents, are doing likewise. Matt conveys godly wisdom on how to teach our children to use and steward their money in a way that conforms them to Christ and His Kingdom, for His glory. Awesome!

GREG BAUMER
Chairman of Generous Giving and coauthor of *God and Money* and *True Riches*

JOHN CORTINES
Director of Generosity at the Maclellan Foundation and coauthor of *God and Money* and *True Riches*

Is there any aspect of our children's lives that will not be impacted by how they view and use the Lord's money and resources? How can we help them develop biblical convictions and practices? Matt, in his humble, relatable way, provides not just the *why*s but the *how*s, with stories and practical suggestions. For those of us endeavoring to impart biblical financial truth, wisdom, and purehearted motivation to our children, this book is an invaluable help. It has immediately become one of my most highly recommended resources for parents.

MARK GRISSOM
National Stewardship Director for Cru

Trusted is full of wise and biblical advice for parents to teach their kids about handling money. I found Matt's writing practical and insightful. It's also entirely relevant and useful for us adults. Read this book and apply it to your life and your parenting, and you and your kids will experience what the Bible describes as the life that is truly life.

TODD HARPER
Cofounder of Generous Giving

An inescapable reality of life is that we're all being discipled by something or someone. The way we think, view the world, and make decisions is being shaped by some force outside ourselves. We can be discipled by Jesus, by our coworkers, by social media, or even by a news channel. This book gives its readers the always-timely reminder that our finances reflect to whom our faith and true allegiance belong. *Trusted* gives parents and children alike a picture of what healthy stewardship looks like as disciples of Jesus.

KYLE IDLEMAN
Senior pastor of Southeast Christian Church and author of *Not a Fan* and *One at a Time*

Teaching our kids to be faithful stewards of God's resources needs to be one of our top priorities as parents. Matt has given us the tools we need to do just that. *Trusted* provides a wonderful biblical foundation with clear direction to build our kids up and prepare them for a lifetime of honoring God with the resources He entrusts them with.

JAMES LENHOFF
National sales director for Good Sense, cofounder of Wealthquest, and author of *Living a Rich Life*

Like all parents, my wife and I want the best for our kids, and we know that money will be a big deal in their faith journey, their relationships, their impact, and so much more. In *Trusted*, Matt provides clear guidance for fostering in your kids a healthy perspective about money and the early money-management habits that will serve them well for the rest of their lives. It's all grounded in Scripture and brought to life with compelling real-life stories. If you put the ideas from *Trusted* into action, you'll make an invaluable investment in the lives of your children.

BOB LOTICH, CEPF®
Author of *Simple Money, Rich Life* and host of the *SeedTime Money* podcast

A truly unique parenting book equipping moms and dads to not only model but also teach their kids the proven principles that lead to financial freedom. I love the combination of good financial counsel and parenting helps (and just enough Chicago stories to make me crave pizza).

JONATHAN MCKEE
Author of over twenty-five books, including *Parenting Generation Screen*

Filled with memorable real-life anecdotes and informed by careful biblical study, *Trusted* is a treasure trove of practical wisdom. I don't know of a better guide to help parents train their children to be wise financial stewards. Matt Bell has done a great service for the church in writing this book.

ROBERT L. PLUMMER, PHD
Collin and Evelyn Aikman Professor of Biblical Studies at The Southern Baptist Theological Seminary

Your children will learn about money from somewhere, and what they learn will significantly impact their lives. As parents, we should be concerned whether the teachings on money our children receive are financially wise and biblically sound. Matt Bell has put together an excellent resource to help parents lead their children in finances. Get it. Read it. And prepare your children to manage money in a manner that avoids common money mistakes and glorifies God.

ART RAINER
Author of *The Money Challenge for Teens* and The Secret Slide Money Club series

I love the vision Matt has for this book—that cultivating within each of our kids biblical financial perspectives and practices will enrich their relationship with Jesus, strengthen their relationship with their future spouse, enable them to make the difference with their life they were designed to make, and so much more. Through solid biblical teaching, practical guidance, and real-life examples, *Trusted* will help you bring that vision to life in your kids.

ROB WEST
CEO of Kingdom Advisors and host of *MoneyWise*

I've always enjoyed reading Matt's material on finances, but this book may be his best and most important work. Everything changes for the good when our kids embrace God's design for managing money. So devour this book. You and your kids will benefit from its biblical grounding and practical application.

ASHLEY WOOLDRIDGE
Senior pastor of Christ's Church of the Valley in Phoenix, Arizona

One of the most important things that we can teach our children about, besides their relationship with Jesus, is how to handle money in a God-honoring way. Our discipleship as parents in this area will impact our children their entire lives. Matt has laid out a game plan that will change your legacy for generations to come. Read it, and more importantly, *do it*! Your kids will thank you one day. We guarantee it.

DAVE AND ANN WILSON
Hosts of *FamilyLife Today* and authors of *No Perfect Parents*

Matt Bell

Giving

Trusted

Preparing Your Kids for a Lifetime of God-Honoring Money Management

Saving

Spending

FOCUS
ON THE FAMILY.

A Focus on the Family Resource
Published by Tyndale House Publishers

For Jonathan, Andrew, and Annika

You are vivid, daily expressions of Psalm 127:3—
priceless gifts, undeserved rewards.
I'm so thankful for you.

"Whoever can be trusted with very little can also be trusted with much."

LUKE 16:10, NIV

Table of Contents

INTRODUCTION More than Money *1*

SECTION I **Stepping Up: The Possibilities and the Perils**
CHAPTER 1 Endless Potential *17*
CHAPTER 2 Growing Up as a Target Market *33*

SECTION II **Stepping In: Seven Money-Management Skills Your Kids Need to Learn before Leaving Home**
CHAPTER 3 Learning to Earn *53*
CHAPTER 4 Planning to Succeed *75*
CHAPTER 5 Living Generously *93*
CHAPTER 6 Saving Patiently *111*
CHAPTER 7 Multiplying Money *129*
CHAPTER 8 Spending Smart *145*
CHAPTER 9 Borrowing Cautiously *163*

SECTION III **Stepping Back: Two Final Lessons for a Healthy Lifelong Relationship with Money**
CHAPTER 10 Our Inner Money Manager *181*
CHAPTER 11 Building God-Honoring Financial Habits That Last *199*

Acknowledgments *213*
Notes *217*

Introduction

More than Money

"For where your treasure is, there your heart will be also."

MATTHEW 6:21

ONE MORNING, when our daughter, Annika, was about three, my wife, Jude, and I heard her getting dressed in her bedroom. With great delight, she exclaimed to no one in particular, "I have pockets!"

We hardly had time to laugh before she followed that with "I want *money* in my pockets!"

Kids develop an awareness of and a curiosity about money at a surprisingly early age. Researchers say that children as young as two can begin to understand that money is a means of exchange. They wouldn't use those words, of course, but when they're with us at the checkout line in a store, they understand at some level that an exchange is taking place. This idea is probably clearer in their minds when we use cash than when we use something as abstract as a credit card or the tap of our phone, but our kids can see that we give the cashier something and we receive something in return—groceries or clothing or a new toy.

Class Is Always in Session

But what are our kids learning about money, and who's doing most of the teaching? If parents are not intentional about teaching their kids wise practices concerning the use of money, the consumer culture that surrounds us will be more than happy to be the teacher. In fact, that culture is teaching all of us all the time—overtly, subtly, and in both cases, very effectively. But the lessons our culture has for us are anything but healthy.

Consider the fact that it's normal for adults to have too much debt and too little in savings, too much financial stress and too little joy. And what about that constant nagging sense that if we just had something more we'd be so much happier? Where did *that* come from?

We have the opportunity to teach our children much better lessons about money, but we have to remember that there's only so much time available. As I write this, our kids are now thirteen, fifteen, and seventeen. In the blink of an eye, our oldest, Jonathan, went from Thomas the Tank Engine to taking the ACT, from coloring books to college visits. When he was born, people told us that time would fly, and now here we are.

While it saddens us to think about our children leaving home, it's also exciting. From the moment they were born, Jude and I understood that our job was mostly to put ourselves out of a job—to prepare our kids to go out into the world and make good decisions on their own. To navigate life's countless ups and downs with faith, perseverance, and wisdom—and have the impact God uniquely designed each of them to have.

I think you'll agree that parenting is filled with moments of great joy and just as many daunting responsibilities. What's more, children don't exactly come with owner's manuals that tell us what to teach them about money or anything else. That's why Jude and I are so grateful for the mentors God put in our lives.

The Funnel

When Jude was pregnant with Jonathan, we took part in a parenting class led by the associate pastor at our church, Keith, and his wife, "Cag" (Caroline). They used the metaphor of a funnel to suggest a helpful way of thinking about raising kids. As Keith explained, "The basic principle is that you start very narrow in terms of what you expect of your kids and the freedoms you give them. During the early years, parents make most of the decisions for their kids— what they'll eat, what they'll wear, who they'll hang out with. As kids get older and prove themselves more trustworthy and capable of making wise decisions, the funnel broadens. Eventually, the goal is for them to be making good decisions on their own."

That metaphor made a lot of sense, and it had the advantage of being biblical! This principle can be seen in the parable of the talents, in which Jesus describes our relationships with God and money by using the story of a wealthy man who entrusts his property to the care of three servants before leaving on a journey: "To one he gave five talents, to another two, to another one, to each according to his ability. Then he went away" (Matthew 25:15).

That's interesting already, isn't it? The master entrusted each of his servants with different talents—units of money—based on their current abilities. In the same way, the amount of money or responsibility we entrust to our children should be based on their current abilities.

> "He who had received the five talents went at once and traded with them, and he made five talents more. So

also he who had the two talents made two talents more.
But he who had received the one talent went and dug
in the ground and hid his master's money. Now after a
long time the master of those servants came and settled
accounts with them." (Matthew 25:16-19)

The two who made something more of what was entrusted to
them were strongly affirmed by the master. He told each of them,
"Well done, good and faithful servant. You have been faithful over
a little; I will set you over much. Enter into the joy of your master" (Matthew 25:21). But the servant who did not do anything
productive with what was entrusted to him was roundly rebuked.
The master even called him "wicked and slothful," telling him that
he should have at least deposited the money in a bank to earn a bit
of interest (Matthew 25:26-27).

This parable contains a few of the foundational principles of
biblical money management that we'll be looking at together in
this book. First, *God owns everything.* Anything in our possession
has simply been entrusted to us by God to be managed according
to His principles and for His purposes. When I read those verses
as a new Christian in my late twenties, they introduced me to a
profoundly new way of thinking about money.

Second, *God expects us to do something productive with what He
has entrusted to us.* We are to manage His resources well.

Third, *as we prove ourselves faithful, God will entrust us with
more.* As we teach our kids about wise money management, and as
they demonstrate their ability to faithfully manage what we entrust
to them, we should entrust them with more. That's how they will
grow in ability and responsibility.

An Incredible Opportunity

It's been my experience that many people misunderstand biblical financial stewardship. They think of it as a heavy burden. They imagine God saying to them, "Here is some of My stuff. Don't break any of it or lose any of it." That seems to be how the third servant understood his master's instructions—and look what happened to him!

But that isn't God's message. Instead, He's saying, "Here's a portion of what I own. Manage it well, enjoy it, use it to do some good in My name, and as you do, I'll give you more to manage." Stewardship isn't a heavy burden; it's an incredible opportunity. Wouldn't it be wonderful if our kids grew up seeing money that way?

One final takeaway from the parable is that someday God will return and we'll need to account for how we managed all that He entrusted to us. That, too, is a good model for us. As long as our kids are under our roofs, they should know they're accountable to us and to God, and when they leave our homes, they will continue to be accountable to God. We're not looking for them to mess up, always ready to scold them for their mistakes. Rather, we're looking for ways to continue teaching them, to give them course corrections as they learn to become wise money managers.

This central principle—that we need to first demonstrate our trustworthiness in small matters before we will be entrusted with more—is reinforced in another parable of Jesus:

> "Whoever can be trusted with very little can also be trusted with much, and whoever is dishonest with very little will also be dishonest with much. So if you have not been trustworthy in handling worldly wealth, who will trust you with true riches? And if you have not been

trustworthy with someone else's property, who will give
you property of your own?" (Luke 16:10-12, NIV)

The two questions that Jesus asks here are ultimately what this book is about. Yes, the chapters ahead will be filled with practical, biblical ideas on teaching our kids about money—giving, saving, investing, spending, and all the rest. But managing money biblically isn't just about managing money. It's very much about our eternal relationships—and our children's eternal relationships—with our Savior, Jesus Christ.

You Can Do This

If you feel hesitant or ill-equipped to teach your children about money, you're certainly not alone. Many parents recognize how important it is that their kids learn about money but are reluctant to be the ones who do the actual teaching. Reasons vary, from a lack of confidence in their own money-management abilities to concerns that they won't be able to teach in a way that resonates with their kids. Others would rather outsource the job to their children's schools.

My encouragement to you? You're the perfect person for this job. Even if you're having some financial struggles of your own or haven't ever studied what the Bible says about money, the fact that you're reading this book shows that you care about helping your kids in this area. That's a huge step in the right direction.

Throughout this book, as I unpack various biblical financial principles, I'm going to focus first on what it can look like for adults to put each principle into practice. Then I'm going to suggest ways we as parents can teach these principles to our children.

I'm also going to encourage you to think about three distinct parenting roles: the gatekeeper, the teacher, and the role model—and how your embrace of each one can be used to foster wise money-management beliefs and behaviors in your kids.

Gatekeeping is about setting rules and defining boundaries. This is about creating and enforcing structural constraints, which are helpful for anyone who's trying to build constructive habits. There's a parenting book that speaks to me about this even though I haven't even read it. It's called *Be the Parent*. The title says it all, doesn't it? Gatekeeping is about stepping up and being the parent. Sometimes it isn't much fun, but it's essential for our children's healthy development.

> *Do not rob your children of limits.*
>
> DR. HENRY CLOUD AND DR. JOHN TOWNSEND, *BOUNDARIES WITH KIDS*

Teaching is about being proactive in conveying particular lessons. Kids aren't born knowing how to prioritize their use of money, how to save or invest it, or how to make smart buying decisions. We have to teach them.

As for being a role model, that's the most important role of all, which is why I'm going to spend time looking at each principle through adult eyes before exploring ways to teach it to our kids. As someone pointed out early in our parenting journey, more will be caught than taught. Our kids will learn the most about money by observation: listening to what we say about money in casual conversations and watching what we do with it. (They're listening more closely and watching more intently than we often realize!) We don't have to have the money thing completely figured out.

We just need to be learning, increasing our understanding of biblical financial principles, and growing in our application of those principles. My hope is that this book will help each of us parents become better money managers, and in doing so, enable us to set powerful, positive examples for our kids.

Ultimately, we want our children to have the wisdom to set their own boundaries and make their own good choices. Some early, proactive gatekeeping and teaching on our part, along with thoughtful, intentional role modeling, will help them get there.

As for our kids' schools, it's great that more and more are doing some teaching in this area. However, studies about school-based financial literacy efforts reveal mixed results at best. Classroom lessons are often too theoretical. Your children's teachers can *talk* about comparison shopping, but you're the one who can take them to a store, show them how you comparison shop, and have them do some comparison shopping of their own. Your children's teachers can *talk* about savings accounts, but you're the one who can help them open a savings account and guide them in building the habit of saving a portion of every dollar they receive. Those real experiences will have a far greater impact on your kids.

The most effective money-management lessons are those that are learned with real money in real time in the real world.

A Living Classroom

When God brought the Jews out of slavery in Egypt, and as He prepared them for all they would experience in their new home in Israel, He stressed the importance of teaching their children about their history. But He didn't tell them to set up a chalkboard and hold classroom sessions five days a week from nine to four. He told them to work their teaching into the natural rhythms of daily life:

"And these words that I command you today shall be on your heart. You shall teach them diligently to your children, and shall talk of them when you sit in your house, and when you walk by the way, and when you lie down, and when you rise. You shall bind them as a sign on your hand, and they shall be as frontlets between your eyes. You shall write them on the doorposts of your house and on your gates." (Deuteronomy 6:6-9)

We would be wise to take the same approach in teaching our kids about money, opening up conversations about it as we go about our daily lives and taking advantage of natural teaching opportunities as they arise.

Mistakes Will Be Made

In the Star Wars movie *The Empire Strikes Back*, there's a scene in which Luke Skywalker is discouraged and doubtful about his ability to lift his X-wing fighter that he crash-landed in a swamp. Spurred on by Yoda, he reluctantly agrees to "give it a try." To which Yoda snaps, "No! Try not. Do, or do not. There is no try."

While it may be presumptuous to challenge a Jedi master, challenge I must. (Sorry!) On the one hand, I get it. We don't want our kids making a feeble attempt at a chore, complaining that it's too difficult, and then giving up. We want them to get the job done. I remember hearing a preacher talk about doing some yard work with his young son. After he asked the boy to pound a stake into the ground, his son complained that the day was too hot and the hammer too heavy. Lovingly but firmly, the dad made it clear that he knew his son could complete the task and expected him to do so. When the boy finished the job, he gained confidence in his ability to do more than what he sometimes thought he could, and he learned about the importance of finishing whatever job he set out to do. *Do, or do not.*

On the other hand, many aspects of money management are rarely so clear. Paying a bill on time might be a matter of do or do not, but when it comes to making a wise purchasing decision, there's a lot of subjectivity involved. And it's in those messier areas where there's much to be learned by trial and error, by trying and failing and trying again. The failing part of that equation is especially important.

The Real World

During a parenting seminar, Dr. Henry Cloud, a renowned Christian psychologist and prolific author, was asked by a mother in attendance, "What is the best thing parents can teach their child?" He said, "I don't know whether there's 'one best thing.' But I can tell you one that's way up there on the list. . . . Teach your child how to lose."

Taken aback, the mother said, "What do you mean, 'Teach him how to lose?' I want my child to win. Why on earth would you want to teach your child how to lose?"

Dr. Cloud explained, "Because he will lose. And since he will, he'd better know how. . . . Losing well, with the ability to continue on, is one of the most important character traits you can develop in your child." Dr. Cloud went on to say, "Your child's ability to do this will determine how well his life goes."[1]

Real losing is far different from getting the wrong answer on a money-management quiz. When a child loses a ten-dollar bill, she feels really bad. That sort of loss can teach her lessons about responsibility like nothing else. Or when a child has a bike stolen after carelessly leaving it on the sidewalk overnight and must go without a bike while saving for a new one.

The key here for parents is to resist the powerful urge we often feel to swoop in and save the day. We must allow our kids to feel some pain, challenge them to solve their own problems, and let them lose well. All of this, of course, should be done in age-appropriate ways and seasoned with grace.

Believe me, I'm saying this as much to myself as to you. I've crossed the line many times and have done too much to "rescue" our kids. But there have also been many times when I haven't, and I know it's in *those* times that they have learned, grown, and gained confidence in their own abilities.

I want our kids—yours and mine—to try lots of things with money. I want them to be hands-on with money, to make some mistakes and to learn by doing. I want them wrestling through the challenge of making trade-offs in the clothing store (one pair of designer jeans or three pairs of not-so-designer jeans?), dealing with the regret of spending their whole weekly allowance right after receiving it, learning to wait as long as it takes to save for something they want to buy, and eventually even experiencing the roller-coaster dynamics of investing money in the stock market. I don't want our kids leaving home just book smart about money; I want them to be street smart.

Keep remembering that the more real-world you make these lessons, the more effective they will be. Teach lessons in real time whenever possible, and have your kids implement the lessons with real money—*their* money. And always remember that you *can* do this.

In fact, you're the best person for the job.

The Road Ahead

The two chapters that make up the first section of this book are designed to give you what I hope will be a very encouraging and exciting sense of all that's possible in teaching your kids about money, as well as an eyes-wide-open look at some of the obstacles that stand in the way. Section two consists of seven chapters, each one focusing on a specific aspect of money management, from earning to planning, and from giving to investing. We'll look at key biblical principles that pertain to each one, spending the first portion of each chapter looking at how to put those principles to work in our own lives—this is essential if we are to be good role models—and then exploring ways to teach each principle to our children. Section three offers more advanced lessons designed to help our kids discover their "inner money manager" and build biblical financial habits that will last.

I recommend that you read the book all the way through so you understand the big picture. Then go back to individual chapters for reminders of how to teach each topic to your kids at various stages of their lives. On my website (mattaboutmoney.com), you'll find my latest recommended tools that will help you implement the ideas in this book.

I'm thrilled that you've decided to embark on this journey. I know your kids will be blessed by your active involvement in this important area of their lives, and I pray that the journey will be a great blessing to you as well.

Recap

If we don't teach our kids about money, it isn't that they won't learn. They *will* learn, but the culture will be their teacher, and what it teaches is often at odds with Scripture. The Bible teaches that God owns everything, He entrusts us with what we can handle right now, and as we prove ourselves trustworthy, He will entrust us with more to manage. That'll be our model throughout the book. When our kids are very little, we make most decisions for them. Over time, as we teach them and as they prove themselves trustworthy, we can and should entrust them with more responsibility. You're the perfect person to use this process in teaching your children God's principles for managing money. Despite any doubts you may have, you can do this!

Stepping Up

The Possibilities and the Perils

CHAPTER I

ENDLESS POTENTIAL

"I came that they may have life and have it abundantly."
JOHN 10:10

In 2012, Jude and I accepted the opportunity for me to join the staff of Sound Mind Investing, which required a move from Chicago to Louisville, Kentucky. As we packed our house, SMI's owner, Austin Pryor, sent a welcome package that contained gifts for our three children. As I quickly discovered, Louisville is big on college basketball, and people who live there are mostly either University of Louisville fans or University of Kentucky fans. Austin is a die-hard Kentucky fan, so the gifts for the kids were T-shirts that celebrated one of Kentucky's recent national championships. Enclosed with the package was a card that contained only the words of Proverbs 22:6: "Train up a child in the way he should go; even when he is old he will not depart from it." (I believe the word *should* was underlined.)

I can't say that we've bought into the "need" to teach our kids which basketball team to cheer for (somehow I'm still gainfully employed), but the longer we've been parents, the more we have seen the larger wisdom in that proverb and the incredible opportunity it represents. The advice pertains to all aspects of parenting, of course, but if we narrow our focus to money, it's exciting to see how helping our kids get on the right financial path could have not just a *linear* effect but an *exponential* effect. Let me explain.

You might be familiar with the concept of compounding, but if not, here's a brief refresher: Compounding is earning interest *on* interest.

Here's an example. If you saved one hundred dollars per month for fifty years and put the money under your mattress, it would grow in a linear fashion (and your mattress would get very lumpy). Each step would be equal to the last. Your hundred-dollar stash would grow to two hundred dollars and then three hundred dollars and on and on. After fifty years, you'd have sixty thousand dollars.

But now let's do something more productive with that money. Let's invest it, and let's assume that over those fifty years you were able to generate the stock market's long-term average annual return of 10 percent. This time your money wouldn't grow in a linear fashion. It would grow exponentially. After fifty years, the sixty thousand dollars you invested would have grown to more than $1.7 million. Wow! That's incredible, isn't it?

Let's take a closer look at how this would happen. In the early days—in fact, in the early years—it wouldn't look like much was happening at all. In the chart below, you can see that after five years, you would have invested six thousand dollars, and it would have earned about another $1,750. That's nice, but nothing too exciting. The amount you invested would have been more than three times greater than the amount you earned. After ten years, you would have invested twelve thousand dollars, and it would have earned about another $8,500. At that point, things would start to get a little more interesting, but still nothing earth-shattering.

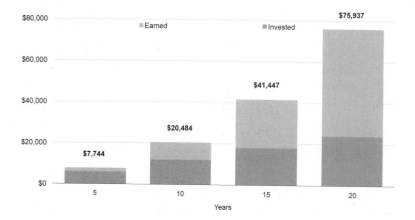

Now let's change the scale so we can allow for more time and account for a lot more growth. Look at the forty-year mark. By then, you would have invested forty-eight thousand dollars, and it would have turned into more than $630,000. Your earnings, more than $580,000, would be more than twelve times greater than what you invested. And take a look at the fifty-year mark, where your sixty thousand dollars would have turned into more than $1,730,000. Your earnings of more than $1,670,000 would completely dwarf the amount you put in. Stunning, right?

The trend line helps show the difference between linear growth and exponential growth. If we were looking at a chart of linear growth, the line would be straight. But an exponential line is far from straight. The further to the right it moves—in other words, the more time you give it—the more steeply upward it bends. At the end, the line is moving almost straight up. That's a very striking

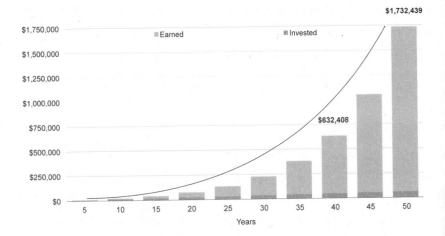

depiction of the power of compounding—or exponential—returns. It's what happens when a return on investment earns a return, and that return earns a return, and on and on.

No Guarantees

Here's an important caveat. The stock market, like life, delivers far from a smooth ride. That last chart used the stock market's long-term average annual return. But that doesn't mean each year's return has been 10 percent. Just look at 2008, when the market fell by more than 37 percent. The next year it rocketed up by more than 28 percent. The following year it gained 17 percent, then just one percent. Or think about what happened in 2020. In February of that year, as the world grappled with the early days of the COVID-19 pandemic, the US stock market fell 34 percent in just sixteen trading days. It had never fallen so far so fast. Then, after bottoming out in the middle of March, the market closed out the year strong.

That 10-percent figure is an *average*—and averages are made up of some years with far greater gains and some with painful declines. To take full advantage of compounding, you have to be patient. You have to stick with it and do the work day in and day out, trusting that one day all your work will pay off. And you have to accept some setbacks along the way—sometimes gut-wrenching, painful setbacks.

Sounds a lot like parenting, doesn't it?

> *Steady plodding brings prosperity;*
> *hasty speculation brings poverty.*
>
> PROVERBS 21:5, TLB

Steady Progress in the Right Direction

Perseverance in doing the right things: This is the principle explained by Jim Collins in his business classic, *Good to Great*, in which he explores the reasons why some companies break away from the pack of their competitors and achieve remarkable, sustained success. While there is usually a point when they do in fact break away, often it is not because of some revolutionary new idea that suddenly shoots them to the top. It's the result of steadily doing the right things over a long period of time.

Collins compares the process to "turning a flywheel," and there's an important lesson here for us parents as we patiently instill lessons of wise money management in our children over many weeks, months, and years.

A flywheel is a heavy disk that helps maintain a constant speed of rotation in a machine or uses its rotation to store energy for other parts of the machine. Collins describes it as "a massive metal disk mounted horizontally on an axle, about 30 feet in diameter, 2 feet thick, and weighing about 5,000 pounds."[1]

Imagine pushing on this thing to try to get it to turn. It takes every bit of muscle you can muster. You push and push. After several hours you get it to make one full rotation. You keep pushing. Eventually, it moves a little faster—a *little* faster. Hours later, you're getting that massive metal disk to make two rotations per hour, but it's exhausting and more than a little discouraging.

People laugh at you. They tell you to stop. They say that whatever you're striving for isn't working. Honestly, at times, even you begin to wonder.

But pushing on the flywheel represents the steps you're taking in pursuit of something that matters to you, like having your kids grow up with a healthy relationship with money. For you, turning a flywheel may not be hard physical labor. It can also be something you're doing little by little over time, often without seeing tangible signs of progress.

Collins found that in all the companies he studied—the ones that achieved unusual success—this was their pattern: In the early years, no one noticed what they were doing. There were no media articles, no shareholder parties. Just a lot of steady plodding, until one day they realized it wasn't taking as much effort. Sales started edging up, and kept going up. The companies started putting distance between themselves and their competitors. Over time, the gap kept getting wider and wider.

The media started calling. Headlines were written about each company's "overnight success." But there was nothing overnight about it. They had been plugging away for a long time.[2]

You'll probably experience something similar as you teach your kids about money. There will be days when you'll wonder whether you're making progress, whether any lessons are sinking in. There will be tough days when your kids make bad choices and then *you* have to make the really hard choice to be the gatekeeper and enforce a boundary.

Keep going. Keep doing the right things. Eventually you'll see some light bulbs turning on, some good and wise decisions being made. You will recognize that as you've been slowly turning this massive flywheel—with the patience and perseverance behind all the lessons you've conveyed—your kids have started to make more decisions on their own. Wiser decisions. And because of the biblical perspective you've brought into your teaching, along with God's goodness in responding to your prayers, He has been shaping their hearts in powerful ways.

While none of us will have the final say in how our kids turn out, I pray and trust that one day we will be stunned by all the good that God brings about in and through their lives.

Immeasurably More

While the application of exponential growth to investing is important (we'll talk more about it in chapter 7) and fairly easy to see, such growth isn't just possible there. Exponential growth is possible in all areas of money management—all the tangible, dollars-and-cents areas of money management, and all the spiritual and character-related areas. And those are even more exciting than the sort of returns you can see on a brokerage statement.

Take generosity, for example. Think about the impact of a child who develops a passion for generosity along with some consistent practices that help her implement that passion. Think about how

God could multiply that exponentially, shaping that child's heart over her lifetime with a deep compassion for the world's many needs and encouraging the habit of making actual difference-making investments to address some of those needs. That child could play a role in saving lives and even shaping eternities. Think about the joy she would experience as a result.

Think about all that a young person could bring to his future marriage by having grown up with a healthy relationship with money. As I'm sure you know, financial issues are a common factor in many divorces. And for couples who stay together, money is often a festering issue that creates stress and tension, robbing them of joy and influence.

On the other hand, a healthy relationship with money can bring a rich sense of satisfaction to a marriage, and that can have an exponential impact that's felt by future generations.

Imagine that your child is now in his forties and has just lost his job. He has a family and a mortgage. His friends try to reassure him, saying, "God will provide." To some people, those words might sound trite. But your son knows it's true. He's been the beneficiary of God's faithful provision before. In the midst of the storm, he actually experiences peace, which ripples out into his marriage and his parenting.

That sort of response doesn't just happen. This perspective doesn't develop overnight. It happens through the steady building of one's faith over time, and a significant part of it can be traced all the way back to when he was a child learning from you some seemingly simple lessons about God's goodness and His promise to provide for us. The calm faith with which he's walking through the job loss is an exponential return on your investment. It's impossible to quantify, but certainly "far more than we would ever dare to ask or even dream of—infinitely beyond our highest prayers, desires, thoughts, or hopes" (Ephesians 3:20, TLB).

Small Beginnings

Later in the book, when I encourage you to have your young children put coins in a piggy bank and you're tempted to think of it as a small thing, I want you to remember this big picture we've been looking at. Because even such a simple lesson as saving a few coins out of every dollar received can have exponential returns. This is true even if you only look at the *financial* benefits of saving money—very few people have enough in savings. Today, something like two-thirds of all Americans live paycheck to paycheck, meaning that they have just enough to pay their bills and cover basic necessities until their next paycheck. That's a stressful, unhappy way to live. It's damaging to a person's health and relationships. And it makes them vulnerable to taking steps backward in their finances, because one unexpected expense can lead them into debt and the feeling that they'll never get ahead. Your kids can live differently. With your help, they can build the habit of saving a portion of all that they earn.

But there's something bigger at stake here. By cultivating the habit of saving money, your kids will be developing a character trait that is foundational to an effective, satisfying life—the ability to delay gratification. Children who at a young age are able to put off an immediate reward to wait for a better one have been found to enjoy an incredible range of benefits later in life, from higher scores on college entrance exams to better relationships. We'll talk more about this in chapter 6. Then, in chapter 11, you'll see that the ability to delay gratification isn't just essential for living a productive, joyful life—it's what will enable your children to experience the healthiest possible relationship with money and to manage it with a deep sense of gratitude, great effectiveness, and an uncommon level of joy.

Even though your kids probably don't have a lot of money right now, and they may be so young that fostering within them some of these bigger-picture perspectives may seem like a stretch, the money-related habits they begin developing right when they first get their hands on some money are extremely important. That's because the financial beliefs and behaviors they learn today, when they don't have much money, will be magnified when they're older and have more. As I discovered firsthand, that's true *for better or for worse*.

Living the Life

As soon as I was old enough to earn money, I did. And I worked hard. When I was twelve, I had a one-hundred-house newspaper route. Every day after school, I'd load up the baskets on my bike and deliver papers until it was dinnertime. We had a gravel driveway, and I remember one day falling as I jumped on my bike to begin that day's deliveries. My knee was cut, with blood dripping down my leg. But I got on my bike and delivered those papers.

When I was fourteen, I got a summer job working in the cornfields owned by one of our town's largest employers, DeKalb Ag, a company that engineered corn and other crop seeds. Early in the morning, I'd walk a couple of blocks from my family's home, wait for a covered pickup truck, jump in the back with a group of other kids my age, get driven out to the fields, and then spend all day walking through rows of corn, either detasseling or cross-pollinating the corn. That was considered a good job because it paid well, but it was hard work under the hot sun.

As I got older, I worked in restaurants and moved my way up from busboy to head cook.

I was very intent on making money, and I was equally intent on *spending* money. When I was sixteen, I bought a car, a good stereo, and more.

In college, those habits were magnified. While working at a radio station on campus, I had to get permission to work all the hours I wanted to work. And I kept spending—on different cars, restaurant meals, and who knows what else.

After graduating from college, my habits of hard work and free spending were further magnified. I discovered credit cards, and I thought they were amazing. I could buy a bunch of things and then pay just a small amount of the bill each month. So I did.

Prodigal Son

In my midtwenties, something completely unexpected happened. I inherited sixty thousand dollars from an uncle. I had no idea he'd planned to leave me any money. It felt like I had won the lottery, and I hadn't even bought a ticket.

Did I use the money to pay off all my credit-card debts? Put some in savings? Start investing? Did I give any of it away? No.

I used the money to create my dream job, producing a newsletter for people who take golf vacations. Once a month, I traveled to some great golf destination—Puerto Rico, southern Spain, the Monterey Peninsula in California. I would play the best courses in the area, take pictures, and write reviews. When I wasn't traveling, I enjoyed myself in Chicago, where I lived, shopping at high-end clothing stores and eating at expensive restaurants. My life was everything I dreamed it could be—except solvent. I was spending far more than I was making each month.

Two years after inheriting the sixty thousand dollars, I woke up to the hard reality that I had spent every last penny of it *and* had racked up twenty thousand dollars of credit-card debt. The habits I'd learned at a young age when I didn't have much money—work hard (good), spend everything I made and then some (not good)—were magnified when I got older, had more money, and gained access to credit cards.

Unable to pay my bills, I completed an unintentional re-enactment of the Bible's parable of the Prodigal Son by moving back home. I went from living the life to living in my parents' basement in the small town where I grew up. While I'll always be thankful to my parents for the safety net they provided, those early weeks were so depressing that all I wanted to do was sleep.

As difficult as that experience was, there were two wonderful life changes that came out of it. First, it made me start to ask some questions about the direction of my life. About that time, I got a call from Wayne, one of my friends from college. I had graduated a year ahead of him, moved out of state for a job, and lost touch with him. Unbeknownst to me, he had become a Christian that year. When he got back in touch, he wanted to talk about his new-found faith. The experience I had been through left me humbled and willing to listen.

Wayne said some tough things, like that the more I had leaned on my own understanding, the more things hadn't worked out so well. I didn't realize it at the time, but he was quoting Proverbs 3:5-6. Wayne also told me some hopeful truths. "God has a plan for your life," he said. Those conversations set me on a path of exploring Christianity.

About eleven months later, now living on my own again, I was on the verge of messing up something else that mattered to me.

Once again I was humbled and broken. Sitting in the quiet of the studio apartment I'd moved into, I bowed my head and prayed a simple prayer: *God, if You really do exist, I'd like to know You. If You really do have a plan for my life, I'd like to know what it is. I'm sorry for the many ways I have surely fallen short of your standards. Thank You for sending Your Son to die on a cross for my sins. From this day forward, please take control and lead my life. Amen.*

A New Beginning

I didn't see any flashes of lightning. There were no visits from angels, no parting of the clouds. But from that day forward, my life began to change in significant ways.

One positive development was that I woke up to my need to learn how to manage money, so I got started. After becoming a Christian, I started attending a church that had a "stewardship ministry" that taught people about biblical money management. I had never heard of such a thing, nor did I realize at the time that the Bible had anything to say about money. It turns out it says a lot.

Since I was deeply in debt and my mismanagement of money was what had led me to Christ, I was fascinated by this ministry. Innocently enough, I asked about serving in it. As a new Christian with twenty thousand dollars of debt, I really should have been served *by* the ministry, but for some reason they let me join the team. Maybe they were short on volunteers.

In order to become properly trained, I needed to attend various financial workshops. I was a sponge, soaking up everything I could. Eventually I was allowed to facilitate discussions at tables of workshop participants. Later I joined the teaching team.

Since I became a Christian at age twenty-nine, there are times when I wish it hadn't taken so long, when I'm tempted to view all the years before that as wasted time. But I know that God has used all the mistakes and foolish decisions I made earlier in life for a purpose.

One benefit of learning financial lessons the hard way is that it has given me a passion for helping young people get onto a good financial path. I want to help people avoid the mistakes I made. It's one reason I love being a parent so much. I'm excited about doing whatever I can to help instill in our kids a passion for walking closely with God, and that includes managing money according to His principles and for His purposes.

I want them to discover as early as possible the "good works" God intends for them to do (Ephesians 2:10), to see and appreciate how He has uniquely designed them and how He plans to use their interests, passions, and abilities to help them live adventurous, difference-making lives. I love how *The Message* paraphrases 1 Corinthians 12:7: "Each person is given something to do that shows who God is." I can't wait to see how that truth gets expressed in each of my children, and I'm sure you feel the same way about yours.

Money can either be a force that helps propel our children toward a life of good works or a roadblock that stands in the way. It's such an important subject in God's eyes that the Bible says more about money than any other topic except the Kingdom of Heaven. In fact, Jesus named money as His chief rival for our hearts when He said, "No one can serve two masters, for either he will hate the one and love the other, or he will be devoted to the one and despise the other. You cannot serve God and money" (Matthew 6:24).

That's such a commonly quoted verse that we risk missing its importance. Why did Jesus mention money there? He could have picked so many other things, all of which can easily distract us from our relationship with Him—our marriages, our work, our hobbies, our friendships. But He chose money.

Get the money thing wrong, and it can shipwreck your life. "For the love of money is the first step toward all kinds of sin. Some people have even turned away from God because of their love for it, and as a result have pierced themselves with many sorrows" (1 Timothy 6:10, TLB).

Get the money thing right, and it can contribute mightily to a life of great joy and impact—a life of being entrusted with increasing responsibilities and increasing opportunities. "His master said to him, 'Well done, good and faithful servant. You have been faithful over a little; I will set you over much. Enter into the joy of your master'" (Matthew 25:21).

Let's help our kids get it right. Let's teach them practical, age-appropriate, biblical lessons of wise money management, and then let's watch with eager anticipation to see how God multiplies those lessons exponentially.

Before we can get to work, though, we need to see very clearly one of our greatest obstacles, and we need to learn some strategies for overcoming it.

Recap

Our kids have an incredibly valuable asset: They have time. Because of the power of compounding, a small amount of money invested over a long period of time can turn into a lot of money. But the incredible multiplying force of compounding isn't restricted to investing. The exponential returns that could be generated through our children as they develop healthy, God-honoring, lifelong financial perspectives and practices around earning, generosity, debt, and so much else are impossible to quantify. Early training in this important area could impact their relationships with Jesus, their relationships with others, and the impact they have in ways that are "far more than we would ever dare to ask or even dream of—infinitely beyond our highest prayers, desires, thoughts, or hopes" (Ephesians 3:20, TLB).

CHAPTER 2

GROWING UP AS
A TARGET MARKET

*"Behold, I am sending you out as sheep in the midst of wolves,
so be wise as serpents and innocent as doves."*
MATTHEW 10:16

WHEN OUR KIDS WERE SUPER YOUNG and I was in an especially
frugal mood, I canceled our cable service and bought an antenna
for our television. I figured that with the money we would save on
cable, the antenna would pay for itself in short order. The problem
is, it didn't work very well. We could only pick up a handful of
channels, including just one kids' channel. While it carried several
shows our kids liked to watch, it also ran the oddest, most age-
inappropriate commercials.

After watching one such commercial on a Saturday morning,
Jonathan, who was four at the time, walked into the kitchen where
I was making breakfast and asked very earnestly, "Daddy, do you
need cash right now?" It was exactly what he had just heard a
celebrity spokesperson ask on a commercial for a payday lender. A
payday lender! On a *kids' channel*! Reassured by my response that
no, I did not "need cash right now," he headed back to the couch.

According to the American Academy of Pediatrics (AAP), children ages seven and younger "have limited ability to understand the persuasive intent (ie, that someone else is trying to change their thoughts and behavior) of the advertiser."[1] In other words, most young kids think commercials are just other programs and believe their messages are true.

With advertising taking on ever more subtle forms, the AAP says that even older kids, including teenagers, "often are not able to resist it when it is embedded within trusted social networks, encouraged by celebrity influencers, or delivered next to personalized content."[2]

This chapter will give you a feel for just how sophisticated, pervasive, and effective marketing has become. It will demonstrate how successful marketers are at shaping the aspirations and behavior of all of us, including our kids. And it will equip you with ideas to help your children successfully navigate our marketing-saturated world.

Always, Everywhere

In Louisville, Kentucky, where my family now lives, there's a United Soccer League Championship team, Louisville City FC. Don't tell them that they're a notch below major-league soccer. They play at a high level, and they utilize equally big-league marketing tactics. At a recent game, almost every pause on the pitch was filled by a promotional pitch. Every yellow card, player substitution, and corner kick—and even the announcement about how many fans were in attendance that night—was "brought to you by . . ." some sponsor. Thankfully, they drew the line at injuries, apparently recognizing that it would be bad form to have a deep-voiced announcer telling the crowd, "This injury time-out is brought to you by . . ." while a player writhed in pain on the field.

The day after the game, while filling our car with gasoline, the small screen on the pump's credit-card reader encouraged me to sign up for a membership rewards program while a larger, full-color screen built into the pump blared commercials for a restaurant and an insurance company. Looking across the street, I saw ads clinging to the side of a fence that enclosed a high-school sports field.

Today, everywhere we turn we see or hear advertising messages, and so do our kids. They're woven into the storylines of shows, movies, and video games. Ads or brand logos are on school scoreboards, school uniforms, and even some school buses. They're all over social media, and they follow us around every site we visit online.

Plenty of marketing messages seem innocent enough. *Okay, so this restaurant has a new chicken sandwich.* Collectively, however, they send a message that isn't so innocent, one that isn't helpful in our quest to manage money well or raise the next generation of wise money managers.

The Greatest Identity Theft Ever

Advertising dates back hundreds of years. Some of it started out as simple text notifications. No, not *that* type of text, but small blocks of simple, factual copy in a newspaper or flyer that told people what products were available where. That began to change in the early 1900s when marketers discovered how to use psychology to sell.

With the advent of mass production came the need for new ways to advertise. In 1916, a speaker told the Nashville Ad Club, "It is all very well to get the sales of things that people want to buy, but that is too small in volume. We must make people want many other things, in order to get a big increase in business."[3]

How does a company make people want "many other things?" Boston College sociology professor Juliet Schor notes that the 1920s marked a turning point: "Of course, ads had been around for a long time. But something new was afoot, in terms of both scale and strategy. . . . Ads developed an association between the product and one's very identity. Eventually they came to promise everything and anything—from self-esteem, to status, friendship, and love."[4]

The overarching marketing message that emerged was what religion historian Joseph Haroutunian described as "being through having."[5] We are what we own. It was around that time that the word *consumer* came into popular use. Earlier, people had been referred to as *citizens* or *workers*.

Today, the word *consumer* is used so often you probably don't give it a second thought. We hear about consumer spending, consumer sentiment, consumer confidence. It may seem like no big deal. However, to *consume* literally means to destroy, use up, or spend wastefully. How's that working out for us?

Consumer isn't just a word; it's a worldview marked by three guiding beliefs:

1. Life is about me—my comfort, my pleasure, my happiness.

2. Happiness is found in money and what it can buy.

3. Life is a competition, a quest for more.

Of course, you and I would not describe our lives' purposes that way. But those are the purposes promoted in our consumer culture. They're largely about fostering a sense of discontent—a sense that I don't *have* enough, that *I'm* not enough. And if we don't notice what's going on, we can find ourselves buying in to a greater degree than we realize.

> *"Larry, how much stuff do you need to be happy?"*
> *"I don't know. How much stuff is there?"*
>
> **"MADAME BLUEBERRY,"** *VEGGIETALES*

While there is no single marketing wizard behind a curtain somewhere pulling levers, our consumer culture holds enormous sway over our lives. It influences how we think about ourselves, what's important to us, what we long for and aspire to, and how we use our time and money. And that culture gets to work on our kids at a surprisingly early age.

Trickle-Down Consumernomics

Growing up with brand imagery all around them, is it any wonder that kids as young as two can identify which cartoon or other characters are associated with endorsed products?[6] Or that by age three, they can recognize an average of a hundred brand logos?[7]

But there's more going on here than brand recognition. A study conducted by researchers at the University of Wisconsin–Madison and the University of Michigan found that marketers' brand *messages* are getting through. "Children as young as three are feeling social pressure and understand that consumption of certain brands can help them through life," said lead researcher Anna McAlister of the University of Wisconsin.[8]

Wait, *help* them? Help them *what*? Fit in? Be part of the "in crowd"? Feel good about themselves?

The consumer culture has communicated its messages through a variety of platforms over the years. The most dominant one today is social media, and it has only amplified those messages.

Critics have long pointed out that social media users don't pay for the product, which means that they *are* the product. By willingly handing over a treasure trove of personal information—not just demographics, but what music and movies they like, where they're dining or vacationing right now, and so much more—they are making it easy for marketers to target and influence them in ways they can't possibly imagine.

But social media platforms are more than venues where young people willingly fill marketer databases with all manner of details about their lives, consume countless hours of content—today's teens spend an average of four hours a day on social media[9]—and buy what they see in influencer videos. Many users eagerly tee themselves up as content. In the documentary *Screenagers*, the mom of a teenage girl says, "She has her tripod, and she has her clicker thing, and now she's just upstairs posing. I haven't seen her take a real photo of anything but herself."

> *I do notice that social media brings out more of what's already inside me—a subtle belief that I am the center of the universe.*
>
> **AMY CROUCH, *MY TECH-WISE LIFE***

When a social media user starts gaining traction, it's affirming for her to draw new followers, get positive feedback, and possibly even monetize posts. For marketers, each person with a large following presents a selling opportunity.

However, for everyone who amasses a large following, there are countless others who try and fail, their every post a plea for affirmation that ends in disappointment or even tears. And that's how social media produces the "*I'm* not enough" message. This feeling used to be solved with a purchase. But discouragement over a post that falls flat and constant comparison to filtered photos and carefully curated lives are problems that can't be solved with free shipping.

Girls use social media more than boys, and New York University social psychologist Jonathan Haidt has pointed out that trend lines for anxiety, depression, self-harm, and suicide among teen and preteen girls began to rise dramatically in the early 2010s, which is when social media became available on mobile devices.

> Gen Z, the kids born after 1996 or so—those kids are
> the first generation in history that got on social media in
> middle school. How do they spend their time? They come
> home from school and they're on their devices. A whole
> generation is more anxious, more fragile, more depressed.[10]

Haidt acknowledges that a definitive causal link between the use of social media among teen and preteen girls and a rise in mental illness among teen and preteen girls can't be claimed, but he finds it plausible that the two are related.

A Barna Group study emphasized the role that the amount of time spent online may play in young people's mental health. It found that 19 percent of people ages thirteen to twenty-one said that they hate themselves, 30 percent said that they are depressed or sad a lot of the time, and 33 percent acknowledged having suicidal thoughts. The percentages were even higher among those who spend four or more hours on their phones every day.[11]

What's a Parent to Do?

Let's start with a reality check. The Bible doesn't say that on the sixth day God made consumers who would destroy, use up, or waste all that He had made during the previous five days. It says that He made man and woman in His image (Genesis 1:26-27). When we placed our faith in Christ, the Bible says we became "a new creation. The old has passed away; behold, the new has come" (2 Corinthians 5:17). Financially speaking, the "old" that *should* have passed away is our materialistic consumer identity. The "new" that *should* have come is our steward identity, or as I prefer to say it, our *wise builder* identity.

In one of His parables, Jesus teaches us about two ways of responding to God's Word, comparing those responses to home builders who build on different foundations:

> "Everyone then who hears these words of mine and does them will be like a wise man who built his house on the rock. And the rain fell, and the floods came, and the winds blew and beat on that house, but it did not fall, because it had been founded on the rock. And everyone who hears these words of mine and does not do them will be like a foolish man who built his house on the sand. And the rain fell, and the floods came, and the winds blew and beat against that house, and it fell, and great was the fall of it." (Matthew 7:24-27)

The rock is God's Word, the sand our consumer culture. The identity of a steward, or wise builder, is completely different from that of a consumer, and it is marked by three very different guiding beliefs:

1. Life is not about *us*; it's about *God*. When the Pharisees asked Jesus what the most important teaching was in the law, He responded, "You shall love the Lord your God with all your heart and with all your soul and with all your mind. This is the great and first commandment" (Matthew 22:37-38).

2. Happiness isn't found in *money and what it can buy*; it's found in *relationships*: "And a second is like it: You shall love your neighbor as yourself" (Matthew 22:39).

3. Life is not about *competition*; it's about *contribution*— making a God-glorifying difference with our lives: "For we are God's handiwork, created in Christ Jesus to do good works, which God prepared in advance for us to do" (Ephesians 2:10, NIV).

Love God. Love people. Make a difference. For the steward—the wise builder who puts God's Word into practice—these are the three main purposes of money. Orienting our use of money toward these primary purposes is the beginning of financial wisdom, the starting point for using money in the most effective, satisfying, God-glorifying way.

But here's the problem. Many of us never got the memo about our financial identity. Maybe *you* are just now hearing about it for the first time. And even once we do get this message, it isn't always easy to live by it. Yes, we became new creations when we accepted Christ as our Lord and Savior (2 Corinthians 5:17), but if we are to live *in* the consumer culture without becoming *of* it (see John 17:14-15), we have to remember who we are and choose to act accordingly. We consciously have to "*put off* [our] old self, which belongs to [our] former manner of life and is corrupt through deceitful desires, and to be renewed in the spirit of [our] minds, and to *put on* the new self, created after the likeness of God in true righteousness and holiness" (Ephesians 4:22-24, emphasis added).

> *Guard your heart above all else,*
> *for it is the source of life.*
>
> PROVERBS 4:23, HCSB

Raising the Next Generation of Wise Builders

As long as our children live under our roofs, we have the responsibility to act as gatekeepers. One way we can guard our kids' hearts is by regulating their screen time. As mentioned above, too many destructive ideas can enter our homes through media, and they aren't limited to consumerist messaging. There are sexual predators online, pornographic and near-pornographic images easily available, people boasting about their use of alcohol and drugs, and lots of opportunities to hear bad language. Plus, social media platforms are intentionally designed to keep people constantly engaged, drawing attention away from kids' more important priorities, like homework and sleep.

For children younger than eighteen months, the American Academy of Pediatrics recommends no screen time other than video chat with family. For those ages eighteen to twenty-four months, the AAP says it's okay to "introduce digital media," but for children up to age five, the group recommends a maximum of just one hour per day and that parents watch shows with their children to help them understand what they're seeing. For children six and older, the AAP recommends parents "place consistent limits on the time spent using media, and the types of media."[12]

That last guideline is pretty vague. What is a reasonable limit? Jonathan Haidt recommends some basic guidelines:

- all screens out of the bedroom thirty minutes before bedtime
- no social media until high school
- time limits on total daily device use, such as two hours per day[13]

I like the idea of establishing screen-free zones in our homes, such as the dining room and bathrooms. In our home, my wife and I do not allow televisions or desktop computers in any bedroom. We allow laptop computers, tablets, and cell phones to be used, but not kept, in bedrooms. The door must be open and the screen visible from the door. We also set limits on the days and hours when screen time is allowed.

We established our rules with conversations and a contract. When our sons, Jonathan and Andrew, received their cell phones (Annika, at age thirteen, doesn't have one yet), they came with a three-page contract. The boys had to initial every point and then sign the document. We also enforce our rules with screen-time controls where we set each night's downtime hours, restrict access to certain apps and sites, and monitor how much screen time is being used per device.

Andy and Catherine Crouch raised their two children maintaining one-hour-a-day, one-day-a-week, and one-week-a-year tech sabbaths. Andy, author of *The Tech-Wise Family*, says, "We are not here as parents to make their lives easier but to make them better. We will tell them—and show them—that nothing matters more to our family than creating a home where all of us can be known, loved, and called to grow. And then we'll have to make hard choices—sometimes radical choices—to use technology in a very different way from people around us."[14]

Truth and Lies

In whatever ways our kids experience our consumer culture, it's important that they learn how to look at it objectively. If your kids are very young, a good first step is to help them understand the distinction between programming and advertisements. Help them recognize advertising when it occurs in apps and video games and other areas of life. When appropriate, analyze the messages in advertising, asking your kids to explain what message is being communicated and whether that message is true. I know of one family that has turned this into a little game they call "identify the lie." As they watch commercials together, they ask their kids what the overall messages are. What's the product or service that's being promoted? What benefits are being promised? Are there any lies being told?

The most important part of helping our kids navigate our consumer culture is to help them recognize what is true. If they understand God's truth, the lies of our culture will be easier to identify and reject. Let's encourage them to "write" God's Word on their hearts (Proverbs 7:3). That means reading God's Word, reflecting on it, memorizing it, and as God told Joshua, meditating on it "day and night, so that you may be careful to do according to all that is written in it. For then you will make your way prosperous, and then you will have good success" (Joshua 1:8). Here are some verses I suggest you start with.

1. "See what kind of love the Father has given to us, that we should be called children of God; and so we are" (1 John 3:1).

   I can still hear the intonation in my friend JT's voice as he referenced this verse in the first Bible study I attended: "What manner of love is *this* that God would call us his children?"

   I would love for our kids to be awestruck by the reality that God knows them by name and loves them unconditionally —for them to know deep in their hearts they are children of God, fully loved no matter what brand of clothing they wear or where we can afford to take them on vacation.

2. "Everything is permissible for me, but not all things are beneficial. Everything is permissible for me, but I will not be enslaved by anything [and brought under its power, allowing it to control me]" (1 Corinthians 6:12, AMP).

   Ask your kids to think of some examples of things that may be "permissible" but not "beneficial." It may be permissible to use social media, but is it beneficial? It may be permissible to follow certain people, but is it beneficial? Then ask: What are some ways that using social media or spending too much time playing video games might not be beneficial?

3. "'Watch out! Be on your guard against all kinds of greed; life does not consist in an abundance of possessions'" (Luke 12:15, NIV).

The world gives us the exact opposite message that Jesus gives us here. According to our culture, we really *are* defined by what and how much we have. Ask your kids to consider these commonly held beliefs. What are the "cool" brands? What have marketers done to make them seem cool?

4. "They exchanged the truth about God for a lie, and worshiped and served created things rather than the Creator—who is forever praised. Amen" (Romans 1:25, NIV).

Ask your kids: Where is the line drawn between liking a brand or product and worshiping it? Between liking certain celebrities and worshiping them?

Marketers are all about fostering a love for the "created things" of this world. That's why they are most effective when they build not just brand awareness but brand meaning, when they capture our hearts and our kids' hearts and convince us that this or that product or brand will make us worthy of love and respect.

We can either live reactively in our consumer culture, bouncing "from one purchase to another like balls in a pinball machine,"[15] or we can live proactively, remembering who we are in Christ.

With marketers eager to reach our kids' hearts, what if that space was already occupied? What if there was no room for the lies "I don't *have* enough" or "*I* am not enough"? What if their hearts were filled to the brim with the truth about who they are?

Giving Thanks

Just as the evil one "prowls around like a roaring lion looking for someone to devour" (1 Peter 5:8, NIV), our consumer culture prowls around looking for those who are vulnerable to the messages that happiness and acceptance can be found in the things they buy.

Gratitude is a very effective antidote. When our consumer culture bumps up against people who are thankful for what they have, it doesn't know what to do with them. Gratitude confuses the culture and takes away its power.

Regularly giving thanks for the many gifts that we often take for granted—our health, food on the table and a roof over our heads, good friends, the stars in the night sky—is good for our souls. As you thank God for these things, ask your kids to pray with you. Regularly naming specific things they are thankful for is a good habit for them to build.

Empowering Our Kids for Wise Choices

Living in our consumer culture requires us to play a great game of defense, but defense will only get us so far. Ultimately, we want our kids to understand what's really going on in our culture and then take ownership of their behavior. As it pertains to online behavior, that means making conscious choices about social media usage, what types of content to post, whom to follow, and how much time to spend online.

One way to build healthy habits is to encourage your teens to turn off notifications. That was one common recommendation at the end of the powerful documentary *The Social Dilemma*. At the very least, limit notifications to a few important sources. Keeping track of all notifications can cause us to spend more time online than we would have otherwise and to view content that we may not have chosen to view otherwise. It's a good suggestion for us adults as well.

The documentary *Screenagers* included comments from several teens trying to navigate a complex online world. One downloaded an app that prevented her from accessing certain websites. Another said that when he goes out to eat with friends, they all lay their phones down on the table, and whoever checks their phone first has to pay for the meal.

After Andy Crouch wrote *The Tech-Wise Family*, his college-age daughter, Amy, wrote *My Tech-Wise Life*. In it, she describes growing up in a tech-intentional family and how this has influenced the decisions that she and her friends make today. One friend uses social media exclusively to encourage friends, another to post art and poetry he likes.

I encourage you to watch *The Social Dilemma* with your kids, as long as they are about eleven or older. After we viewed this movie, each of our kids chose certain boundaries that we had not previously imposed on them. There's something powerful about hearing about the dangers of social media from people who have worked for some of the most prominent social media platforms.

Walking the Talk

"I saw this often: adults setting limits for their kids, but not wanting limits for themselves." That's Dr. Delaney Ruskin, the filmmaker behind the two *Screenagers* films. "Can we really tell our kids to do as we say, not as we do?" Great question.

I'm not sure what's more difficult: Setting and enforcing screen-time limits for our kids or setting and following them ourselves. And yet we must.

Not that it's easy. There is always one more email or text message to respond to, one more notification to draw our attention. But I'm convinced that one of the greatest ways we can express love to our kids is to set a good example in the use of technology. To close our laptops by a certain time every night. To not allow a buzzing phone to draw us away from dinner. We will all benefit from a little less FaceTime and a little more face time.

We'll return to the important role that identity plays in how we and our kids think about and use money toward the end of this book. But first we're going to get really practical by looking at all the ways we can wisely manage money and how we can teach our kids to do the same.

Recap and Next Steps

Advertising and marketing messages are all around us. Our consumer culture conditions us to believe that life is about us, that happiness comes from money and what it can buy, and that life is a competition to have more. Again and again, we are taught that we don't *have* enough and *we* are not enough. Of course, the truth is very different. Life is about God, happiness comes from relationships, and life is about contribution. Cultivating within our kids this biblical worldview will take both a strong game of defense and a strong game of offense.

- When they are very young, help your kids distinguish between programming and commercials. As they get older, help them learn to objectively evaluate marketing messages. Can they identify any lies?

- As early as middle school, encourage your kids to notice the use of the word *consumer*. Ask them to look up its definition,

and then discuss how the worldview of a consumer dif-
fers from that of a steward (or manager) of someone else's
possessions—God's possessions.

- Establish clear screen-time rules, enforce the boundaries you
  set, and model good habits.

- As they get older, decide if and when your kids can use social
  media. Set some parameters and eventually help them make
  their own good choices—what content they will post and
  what content they will take in.

- Watch *The Social Dilemma* together and discuss it as a family.

- Proactively cultivate the practice of gratitude in your family.

- As soon as your kids are old enough to memorize Scripture,
  encourage them to memorize 1 John 3:1: "See what kind
  of love the Father has given to us, that we should be called
  children of God; and so we are."

Stepping In

Seven Money-Management
Skills Your Kids Need to Learn
before Leaving Home

CHAPTER 3

LEARNING TO EARN

Whatever you do, work at it with all your heart, as working for the Lord,
not for human masters, since you know that you will receive an inheritance
from the Lord as a reward. It is the Lord Christ you are serving.

COLOSSIANS 3:23-24, NIV

I ONCE HEARD the late Habitat for Humanity ministry founder Millard Fuller tell a moving story about former president Jimmy Carter. After leaving office, Carter and his wife, Rosalynn, spent countless hours volunteering with the ministry, helping build houses for needy families. At one such house, Fuller asked a little boy who was part of the family who lived there if he knew who built his house. Expecting him to credit President Carter, the little boy happily surprised him by exclaiming, "Jesus built my house!"

Doesn't that paint a great picture of the work of a Christian? Whether it's the job we do for a living or the work we do as a volunteer, wouldn't it be wonderful if the world caught a glimpse of Jesus in the way we work? And wouldn't it be great if we could instill such habits, attitudes, and motivations in our children?

A Biblical View of Work

Work was God's idea. He worked in creating the world, and since we were made in His image, work is central to our design. When God put Adam to work in the idyllic Garden of Eden, He gave him a meaningful job to do, tending and caring for God's creation (Genesis 2:15). When Adam and Eve sinned against God, the nature of work changed, introducing an element of toil (Genesis 3:17). All of us experience that from time to time. But work still plays a vital role in our lives.

Much like the way our culture declares so many falsehoods about money and possessions, it also has its own messaging about work. The world says our work is all about *us*—our position, our pay, and our perks. Our jobs define who we are. In God's economy, though, things look very different. Work is a central vehicle through which we can express the three purposes of a wise builder that we looked at in the previous chapter. Work is a platform for living out the others-centered lives we were designed to live, bringing glory to God, loving others, and making a difference in the world.

Let's take a closer look at work through adult eyes first, and then we'll explore ways to teach our children how to work well.

Glorifying God through Our Work

What exactly is Christian work? Is it only the work done by someone in full-time ministry, such as a pastor or missionary? Dorothy Sayers, a British writer and theologian, defined it in this wonderfully simple way: "The only Christian work is good work well done."[1] In other words, as long as the product or service at the heart of our work isn't at odds with God's purposes, the Christian's work can encompass a wide variety of jobs. What matters is the excellence with which we do our work, as Martin Luther King Jr.

said so powerfully in a 1967 speech to students at a junior high school in Philadelphia:

> Even if it falls [to] your lot to be a street sweeper, sweep streets like Michelangelo painted pictures. Sweep streets like Beethoven composed music. Sweep streets like Leontyne Price sings before the Metropolitan Opera. Sweep streets like Shakespeare wrote poetry. Sweep streets so well that all the hosts of heaven and earth will have to pause and say, "Here lived a great street sweeper who swept his job well."[2]

Doing our jobs well means so many things. It means doing them with skill and care, with a good attitude and a desire to honor God. And it means working with humility, holding your job with gratitude to the One who gave the work to you:

> "Beware lest you say in your heart, 'My power and the might of my hand have gotten me this wealth.' You shall remember the LORD your God, for it is he who gives you power to get wealth, that he may confirm his covenant that he swore to your fathers, as it is this day." (Deuteronomy 8:17-18)

Today there's a lot of talk about "building your personal brand." It's true that it can be good stewardship to be intentional about strengthening our résumés and managing our careers. However, we would be wise to remember that our work isn't about drawing attention to ourselves but drawing attention to God.

How differently we might work some days if we remembered

more often that the quality of our work—our attitude toward it and the motivation behind it—could show others who God is.

Loving People through Our Work

When I think back on various jobs I've had, my fondest memories aren't of the projects I've been involved in. They're of the people I worked with. I remember one person I reported to who would introduce me to others by saying, "This is Matt. He works with me." Not *for* me, but *with* me. Such a seemingly small thing, yet it made a big difference. I remember another one who was incredibly smart and good at what he did, yet very humble and completely without pretense. He valued his team before he valued productivity. We knew that he cared about us, which is why we worked so well together and, yes, got a lot of work done.

Our work provides countless opportunities to love people. Everyone has something going on beneath the surface of what we can see. We would be wise to remember this the next time a customer complains or a coworker seems uncharacteristically quiet. Something deeper might be going on there, and the wise and godly worker is always sensitive to that possibility, responding with kindness. Yes, we have jobs to do, but how we interact with the people in our midst while doing our jobs matters even more.

Making a Difference through Our Work

In Jeremiah, we read these instructions from God: "But seek the welfare of the city where I have sent you into exile, and pray to the LORD on its behalf, for in its welfare you will find your welfare" (Jeremiah 29:7). Christians are also in exile. This world is not our home; our "citizenship is in heaven" (Philippians 3:20). And yet, while we are here, we are to seek the good of our communities.

For some of us, our work may directly enhance the well-being of our communities, as is true for police officers and plumbers, doctors and day care workers. For all of us, the fruits of our labor can be used for the good of those around us. For example, by spending money locally, we provide for the livelihoods of local business owners and their employees.

A healthy, biblical view of work is not one where we seek primarily to profit from our work but to *provide* from it. It's how God lovingly designed us to live. In seeking the welfare of our communities, we find *our* welfare.

Raising the Next Generation of Godly Workers

As you observe your kids, whether it's your three-year-old helping you clean up a spill or your thirteen-year-old learning how to cook, it may feel like a stretch to think about them using their work to glorify God, love others, and make a difference in the world. And yet, under our tutelage, that's exactly what they're training for. Here are some ways to mentor them toward those ends.

Train the Trainer

For many years, parenting styles have been put under the microscope. What is the best way to raise kids? What do they really need? In 2001, the president of the Society for Research on Adolescence declared that no further study was needed. The benefits of "supportive and demanding" parenting were indisputable. Though commonly known as *authoritative parenting*, University of Pennsylvania psychologist Angela Duckworth prefers the term *wise parenting* in order to avoid confusion with *authoritarian parenting*. "Over the past forty years," Duckworth says, "study after carefully designed study has found that children of psychologically wise parents fare better than children raised in any other kind of household." As the graphic below conveys, wise parenting is about setting high standards for our kids within a warm, respectful environment.[3]

The authoritative (or wise) style of parenting applies to coaches and teachers as well. In one experiment cited by Duckworth, seventh-grade student essays were reviewed, marked up by their teachers, and then divided into two piles. Half the students received their essays back with this note attached: "I'm giving you these comments so that you'll have feedback on your paper." The other half received this "wise" note with their work: "I'm giving you these comments because I have very high expectations, and I know that you can reach them." All the students were then given the option to revise their essays. Twice as many of the students who received the "wise" feedback chose to go the extra mile and rework their papers.[4]

This high-standards/high-support approach is similar to the advice given by Christian psychologist Henry Cloud. When a child pushes back because a job seems too difficult or a consequence unfair, we should express empathy (a warm, supportive environment) *and* hold firm (high standards). "This is a law of the universe," Cloud explains:

> Frustration and painful moments of discipline help a child learn to delay gratification, one of the most important character traits a person can have. If you are able to hold the limit and empathize with the pain, then character ("the harvest of righteousness") will develop. But if you don't, you will have the same battle tomorrow: "A hot-tempered man must pay the penalty; if you rescue him, you will have to do it again" (Proverbs 19:19).[5]

As an example, Cloud recalled an experience from his own childhood. When he was in the sixth grade, he missed a month of school due to an illness. When he returned, he was overwhelmed with how much work he had to do. One day, he told his mom that it was too much work and he didn't want to go to school.

He can still remember her response: "'Sometimes I don't want to go to work either. But I have to go.' Then she hugged me and told me to get ready for school." Today, Cloud believes, without her example of maintaining clear standards and boundaries, "my life would be full of half-done projects and unfulfilled goals."[6]

As we help our kids build a strong work ethic, we will have frequent opportunities to warmly maintain high standards and to empathize as we enforce limits.

Everyone Works

As soon as they are physically able, all kids should work. The earliest form of work is helping out around the house. As a member of the family, a child should understand that the family can only function well when everyone pitches in. Establishing work as a given is an expression of our gatekeeper role and is a good starting point for helping our kids become diligent workers. Our attitude should be something like *Of course everyone in this family works.* And some of this work is to be done without pay.

Recall the parenting class my wife, Jude, and I participated in, led by Keith, the associate pastor at our church, and his wife, Cag. Each of Keith and Cag's four children grew up doing small jobs. "We wanted to instill in them the idea that we have to pull together as a team," Cag said. "You have to do your part and serve others in the family." At first, that meant helping with the laundry, pairing up socks of same pattern or color. Soon enough, they were setting the table and helping with the dishes.

James and Amanda, a couple in our small group, maintain three lists of chores for their five children: those they must do and for which they are not paid (such as making their beds), those they must do but for which they are paid (such as clearing the dishwasher), and those they could do in order to be paid more (such as yard work).

For ideas on how you can successfully establish a chore system in your home, Focus on the Family offers a helpful list of chores kids can handle at various ages.[7] For example, children ages two or three are capable of taking their dirty clothes to the laundry basket. Somewhere between ages eight and eleven, they can learn to use the washer and dryer on their own.

Chores are not just essential in managing all the work of a household—they are essential to a child's development. A University of Minnesota study found a clear connection between a child's work habits and future success. According to the study's authors, a child "who does chores has a greater chance of success in life," with *success* defined as having quality relationships, finishing their education, not doing drugs, and getting started in a career. In her book *How to Raise an Adult*, Julie Lythcott-Haims explains that people who are most successful in life "began doing chores at three to four years of age."[8]

> *Lazy people want much but get little,*
> *while the diligent are prospering.*
>
> PROVERBS 13:4, TLB

The Work-Pay Connection

The topic of allowances can get surprisingly contentious. On one end of the allowance spectrum are parents who don't believe in the idea. They point out that in life no one is going to just give our kids money; they have to earn it. So they require certain chores of their kids for no pay and then they provide jobs their children can do if they want to earn money. Or, like James and Amanda, in addition to the chores their kids have to do for no pay, there are two levels of paid chores—mandatory and optional.

Pastor Keith and Cag raised their four kids on a no-allowance system where there were mandatory no-pay jobs and optional for-pay jobs. From a young age, their kids' eagerness to earn prompted them to get outside-the-family jobs, delivering newspapers early in the morning before school, mowing lawns, babysitting, and working in a sandwich shop. Cag credits this system for instilling within each of their kids a "massive work ethic."

That's been James and Amanda's experience as well. "Our fifth grader will ask me, 'Can I do this chore? I'm saving for something,'" James said. "That's been great to see, as opposed to, 'I'd like this. Can you buy it for me?'"

In our home, our kids have long been expected to do their part around the house *because they're part of the family.* That means taking turns setting the table, clearing the dishwasher, vacuuming, and more. We also provided an allowance for each of our kids beginning at age five *because they're part of the family.*

The size of the allowance was enough to help them learn some early lessons about managing money, such as how to set aside portions for giving and saving. At the same time, we made sure the amount we gave wasn't enough to buy very much. If they wanted something more expensive, they needed to earn the money by doing extra chores.

At age twelve, their allowance ended. We figured they were old enough to do bigger paid jobs, either for us or for others, such as mowing lawns or caring for neighbors' dogs. They are still required to do certain chores because they are part of the family and are still expected to give and save, but these actions now flow out of their early training and their own initiative.

Keep the Big Picture in Mind

There are a few interrelated learning experiences going on here:

- cultivating within our children a strong work ethic
- bringing money into the equation to help them connect payment with a job well done
- giving them hands-on experience managing money

There is no single correct way to get money into our kids' hands. Some families provide an allowance. For others, that word must never be spoken; the only way to receive money is to earn it. I know of kids raised under both systems who have turned out just fine. So don't stress over this point or think that you have to choose the perfect and right answer to this question. Instead, prayerfully decide with your spouse what sort of chore/money system you will set up. Then implement your plan and stay with it. Whatever you decide, here are some ways we can cultivate within our kids a God-honoring work ethic and help them make the work-pay connection.

Own the Work

While writing this book, I went to see my friend and longtime mentor Dick Towner and his wife, Sibyl. As I pulled into the 150-acre Christian retreat center that they had assumed responsibility for in their "retirement," Dick, at age eighty-three, was shoveling sand as it poured from a dump truck. The property looked as beautiful as ever. Dick, who can outwork a person half his age, still does a lot of the work himself.

Dick was raised by his grandparents. Over lunch, he recalled a time when he was about fourteen and his grandfather had put him in charge of mowing the lawn. One morning, when the lawn clearly needed mowing, Dick had other things he wanted to do away from home. When he returned late that afternoon, he was horrified to see that the lawn was freshly mowed. When he asked his grandfather who had mowed the lawn and why, his grandfather didn't scold him. He simply explained that the job had needed to be done so he'd done it himself.

Dick felt horrible that his grandfather had felt compelled to do the work that was Dick's responsibility. From that day forward, he made sure to mow the lawn right when it needed to be mowed.

As I mentioned, Dick was eighty-three years old when he told me that story. Clearly, the lessons learned in childhood can make a lasting impression! And what an important lesson for our kids to learn. Developing a sense of ownership of their different chores will serve them well for the rest of their lives.

Finish the Work

Extracurricular activities can also be a good training ground for building a strong work ethic and more. In fact, Duckworth says, "There are countless research studies showing that kids who are more involved in extracurriculars fare better on just about every conceivable metric—they earn better grades, have higher self-esteem, are less likely to get in trouble, and so forth."[9]

When our kids express an interest in a particular activity, if we help instill in them the discipline to stay with it, it will be a foundational learning opportunity for them. I think of Collins, a five-year-old who told her parents, Matt and Jacquelyn, that she wanted to play soccer. They signed her up, but her enthusiasm soon began to wane. There were days when she didn't want to go to practice. Sometimes after arriving for practice, she just wanted to sit in the shade and watch. Matt and Jacquelyn lovingly but firmly told her that she had signed up and needed to participate. They said, "You expressed that you want to play, and now there are people counting on you. Your teammates need you in order to have a complete team. We need you to show up and give all the effort you're capable of."

In another case, Zach, now an adult, vividly remembers a similar experience from his childhood. The summer after his sixth-grade year, having never played football, he joined his middle school team at the encouragement of a friend. Even though he was one of the smaller kids on the team, the coach put him on the offensive line. From the start, things did not go well. One night after telling his parents he wanted to quit, they told him the same thing Matt and Jacquelyn told their five-year-old daughter: We finish what we start. The next morning, as he reluctantly prepared for practice, Zach found this note from his dad on the breakfast table.

Zach,

Read the following Scriptures this morning:

- *Philippians 4:13 (strength)*
- *1 Peter 4:10–11 (strength)*
- *1 Peter 1:6–7 (perseverance)*
- *2 Samuel 22:33 (strength)*
- *Psalm 46:1*
- *Hebrews 11:32–34*

We are proud of you, and I am very confident you can see this through. Have a great practice.

Love,
Dad

With that encouragement, Zach finished out the season. Married and with a young child of his own now, Zach has kept his dad's note all these years. It's a life lesson he has leaned on several times since that summer after sixth grade, and he's intent on passing it down to his son when he gets older.

> *For the moment all discipline seems painful rather than pleasant,*
> *but later it yields the peaceful fruit of righteousness*
> *to those who have been trained by it.*
>
> **HEBREWS 12:11**

Do the Work Well

In helping our kids develop a strong work ethic, money can be used both as a reward and a consequence. Parents Leo and Natalie created a system where they paid specific amounts of money for specific jobs. If a job wasn't completed or wasn't completed well, there was initially grace and correction. But if the issue persisted, on payday, their girls would get a bill.

"We felt that giving them bills was more real-world than reducing their pay," Natalie said. "We would tell them, 'Now someone else has to do your job, so that's going to cost more than if you had done it.'"

You may not give your child an actual bill for avoiding a chore or not doing it well, but the lesson here is important. As our kids work on chores and homework and other jobs, they need to recognize the difference between a quick, half-hearted attempt and an honest effort to do the job well.

Do the Work without Complaint

As we teach our kids the value of work done well, it's important to help them understand the attitude that God expects of us as we "do all things without grumbling or disputing, that [we] may be blameless and innocent, children of God without blemish in the midst of a crooked and twisted generation, among whom

[we] shine as lights in the world, holding fast to the word of life" (Philippians 2:14-16).

In James and Amanda's household, their expectations for good attitudes and strong effort while doing chores has sometimes meant that mandatory work-for-pay jobs have become mandatory work-for-*no*-pay or work-for-*less*-pay jobs. According to Amanda, "For clearing the dishwasher, they might get one dollar if they work really hard or fifty cents if they complain about it."

This is an important lesson for our kids to learn. We must help them recognize that doing a job—even if doing it reasonably well—while complaining about it is not a healthy, biblical approach to work.

Teach the Skills

Work is a perfect vehicle for the funnel concept we looked at in the introduction to this book. Remember that my pastor friend, Keith, and his wife, Caroline, used the metaphor of a funnel to talk about raising kids. Parents naturally start very narrow with what they expect of their kids and the freedoms they allow. As kids get older and prove themselves to be more capable, the funnel broadens out. Eventually, the goal is for our kids to be making good decisions on their own.

When teaching good work habits, the first jobs we give our kids are simple, like sorting socks or putting their clothes away. But even though the tasks are simple, we're still teaching important habits: "Put blue socks with other blue socks." "T-shirts go in the top drawer." Over time, we widen the funnel, providing more sophisticated training and raising expectations. By a certain age, our kids should know whose socks are whose. Eventually, they should be doing their own laundry.

The process requires teaching kids how to do the job and then slowly backing off. Julie Lythcott-Haims credits one of her friends with suggesting this progression: "First we do it *for* you, then we do it *with* you, then we watch *you* do it, then you do it completely *independently*."

When Dick and Sibyl were raising their two boys, Sibyl learned quickly the importance of being specific: "'Clean your room' could be somewhat abstract. It's based on your perspective of what you think a clean room is. 'Make your bed' worked better. It was specific enough that you could know if it was done—a bed is either made or unmade." She also found that expecting a bed to be made somehow naturally led to a room being kept neater overall than it would have been otherwise.

Connect Work to Values

Dick and Sibyl are also proponents of tying behavior to values. For example, they emphasized not leaving dishes in the sink. "Either wash it or put it in the dishwasher," Sibyl says. "That way, you're always thinking about the next person. You don't like to come to a messy sink, and neither does the next person. This is a value we have as a family, and it spreads out to other places. If you go down to the laundry room and something is in the dryer, fold it."

Work is indeed one way we live out the values we have as a family. Help your children connect the dots between jobs done well and the reasons we do those jobs to begin with—to bring glory to God and show love to others through our work.

Trust

When I was sixteen, I got a job at a steakhouse and worked my way up to being the head cook. I loved working there, largely because of the boss, J. P. Morgan. (No kidding, that was his real name.) J. P. made sure we were trained well, and then he trusted us to do our jobs.

I can remember many nights when there would be a line of customers out the front door, a stack of orders in my hand, and steaks all over the grill. Without fail, J. P. would walk down the line and say, "Mr. Bell, is there anything I can do for you?" I loved that. It spoke volumes about how much he trusted me to get the job done and get it done well. And that trust made me want to work even harder for him. I would have waxed the underside of his car in a snowstorm if he'd asked me to.

Contrast that with the restaurant chain's regional manager, Bob (not his real name). If Bob was in town, and we had an especially busy night, he would walk down the line, silently grab a pair of tongs, and start moving steaks around. I hated that. It spoke volumes about his apparent lack of trust in me. It was completely demotivating.

That's a lesson I've tried to remember as we teach our kids how to do various jobs around the house. Teach and then *trust*. Our kids don't mow the lawn exactly like I do, and that's okay. As long as they avoid running over the rebar sticking out of the ground near a utility box, it doesn't matter to me where they start or what direction they mow.

We teach and then trust, which helps kids make the job their own.

Work around Home

Sometimes, especially if I don't know *how* to clearly teach a certain job, I'll go straight to trust. Recently, the handle on one of our closet doors stopped working. After buying a new one, I was about to open the package, read the instructions, and attempt to replace it myself. I'm not the handiest guy on the block, so I figured it might take an afternoon.

But I stopped myself, deciding this task would be a good learning opportunity for Andrew, who was fourteen at the time. Still, some micromanager tendencies tempted me to open the package and read the instructions first and then supervise his work, but resisting that temptation, I handed him the unopened package, challenged him to figure it out, offered him five dollars for the job, and got out of the way. He had the handle installed in no time, learning a simple handyman skill all people should probably know (although I still don't) and gaining a lot of confidence and satisfaction in the process.

Work away from Home

There is much value to having our kids work outside the home as well. One summer, a couple named Larry and Amanda kindled an entrepreneurial fire in their eleven-year-old twin boys by encouraging them to start a lawn-mowing business. "It's hard to teach a kid about business if they're not *doing* business," Larry explained. Soon enough, the boys had quite a few customers. "They're having conversations with adults. They're learning about doing good work, having a good work ethic. They're asking the right questions: *How do you split the money? How do you keep a ledger?*"

The boys also gained confidence by knocking on doors, asking for work, and negotiating prices. What's more, they developed the persistence and thick skin needed to deal with rejection.

Another benefit of working for someone else is that other leaders, whether they're bosses, coaches, or music teachers, might be better at holding our kids to a high standard. In her book *Grit*, Angela Duckworth tells the story of a girl who was late to school "almost every day." Then one summer, the girl got a job at a clothing retailer. On her first day, the store manager said, "Oh, by the way, the first time you're late, you're fired." The girl was stunned. No second chances? All her life, there had been patience, understanding, and second chances.

So what happened? Duckworth reports that the girl's father was amazed by the change she made. "Quite literally, it was the most immediate behavior change I've ever seen her make," he said. Suddenly his daughter was setting two alarms to make sure she was on time, or early, to a job where being late was simply not tolerated.[10]

The Roots of Possibility

Children have amazing potential. Have you ever considered what that looks like financially? If they start their career around age twenty-one or twenty-two with a fifty-thousand-dollar salary and earn a 2-percent raise each year, by the time they're seventy they will have earned more than four million dollars.[11] That represents an incredible opportunity to provide well for their families and make significant Kingdom investments.

Of course, earning that kind of money over one's career is far from certain. There's no such thing as guaranteed employment anymore, but there *is* something very close to guaranteed *employability*. The work habits and attitudes we've discussed in this chapter will always be in demand.

But there's much more at stake here. Through the quality of their work, the attitude they bring to their work, and the motivation that drives their work, our kids can bring glory to God, love others well, and make a great difference in their communities and the world. And the foundation for all that can be built when they're young.

Let's look for opportunities to integrate these foundational ideas into our interactions with our kids. Let's help them see that doing their jobs well is glorifying to God, that taking out the garbage and mowing the lawn is a way of loving their family, and that running a lemonade stand isn't just about making money—it's about valuing community and seeking the welfare of their neighborhood on a hot day.

Recap and Next Steps

Work is a central platform for loving God, loving others, and making a difference. Those are three overarching biblical motivations for our work. It isn't something we are primarily to profit from but to provide from. It's even an avenue through which we can show others who God is. Ideally, that perspective will inspire us to do our work with excellence and with a good attitude. In order to cultivate within our kids a God-honoring, diligent work ethic, an authoritative (or wise) parenting style will help, where we set high standards and help our kids meet those standards in a warm, supportive environment.

- As soon as they are able to, all kids should work. Everyone must do their part to help out around the house.

- Decide how you will combine work with pay. Will you use an allowance? Will it be tied to chores? If so, what combination of jobs for no pay and jobs for pay will you utilize? What's important is to choose your system and then implement it with consistency.

- Some key work lessons to teach our kids include: (1) owning the work (which can be learned when they have some ongoing responsibility, such as cleaning a bathroom weekly), (2) finishing the work ("We finish what we start"), (3) doing the work well (because there's a difference between completing a job and completing it with excellence), and (4) doing the work without complaint ("In everything you do, stay away from complaining and arguing . . ."; Philippians 2:14, TLB).

- Be intentional about teaching your children how to do more and more and then entrusting them with more and more responsibility—move them along from sorting socks to folding clothes to doing their own laundry.

- Encourage your kids to memorize Colossians 3:23-24: "Whatever you do, do your work heartily, as for the Lord and not for people, knowing that it is from the Lord that you will receive the reward of the inheritance. It is the Lord Christ whom you serve" (NASB).

CHAPTER 4

PLANNING TO SUCCEED

The plans of the diligent certainly lead to profit,
but anyone who is reckless certainly becomes poor.
PROVERBS 21:5, HCSB

I SOMETIMES ASK WORKSHOP PARTICIPANTS, "If a budget were a person, who would it be?" Common answers have included Scrooge, the Grinch, Darth Vader, and even the devil. One guy in a class for married couples said, "My mother-in-law."

Clearly, budgets have an image problem.

People who don't use a budget often cringe at the mere mention of the word. They think of a budget as something you *go on*, like a diet. "We can't go skiing this winter—we're *on* a budget." They think of a budget as being about *less*—less freedom and less spending.

And less fun.

If that's you, I'd like you to rethink the dreaded *B* word. A budget isn't something you go on. It's a tool you use to proactively manage money. And it isn't about *less*. It's about more—having more knowledge about where your money is going so you can be more intentional in how you use it and have more for what matters most.

A budget, or as I prefer to call it, a *cash-flow plan*, is the single most powerful tool anyone can use to manage money well.

For some families, using a cash-flow plan helps get their finances under control. Seeing—perhaps for the first time—how much they actually spend on food, entertainment, or clothing can be a shocker. The plan provides the essential information needed to live within their means and find the money to fast-track the payoff of debt or save for a house.

For others, a budget can provide financial freedom. Laura grew up in a home where there never seemed to be enough. With four siblings, a schoolteacher dad, and a stay-at-home mom, money was always tight. After graduating from college, even though she made good money, her automatic reaction to most spending decisions was that she couldn't afford it. She always bought the least expensive version of whatever she was shopping for.

When she married Bill, Laura brought those same ways of thinking with her. However, after Bill introduced her to the simple spreadsheet budgeting system he was using, she was amazed to discover that in many cases, they actually *could* afford it, whether "it" was a more expensive brand of shoes or a nice Sunday brunch. Knowing the truth that they actually had some margin in their cash flow was very freeing for her.

To the degree that it helps you manage money wisely, using a budget may even strengthen your marriage. According to Jeffrey Dew, an associate professor of family, consumer, and human development at Utah State University, money management is a big factor in the health of a marriage. Dew observes that a husband or wife's opinion of their spouse's money-management habits can have a major impact on "the quality and stability" of the relationship:

When individuals feel that their spouse does not handle money well, they report lower levels of marital happiness. They are also more likely to head for divorce court. In fact, in one study, feeling that one's spouse spent money foolishly increased the likelihood of divorce 45 percent for both men and women. Only extramarital affairs and alcohol/drug abuse were stronger predictors of divorce.[1]

As you might have guessed, I believe in the benefits of budgets. I can't imagine living without one. If you don't use a budget, I hope this chapter will motivate you to start. I know a budget will be helpful to you, and it'll be invaluable to your children. Teaching them how to budget—and modeling a positive approach to budgeting—will equip them to manage money effectively. It may even contribute to their happiness within marriage in the future.

Setting Goals, Making Plans

Just in case you're not convinced about this whole budgeting thing, the graphic below might help.

Think about a person in the lower right quadrant. They have no goals and no plan. What are they doing? *Wandering,* right? They don't even know where they want to go. They're living reactively, not proactively.

What about a person in the lower left quadrant? They don't have any goals or destination in mind, but they *do* have a plan, and they're tracking their cash flow. What are they doing? They might be *obsessing,* crunching numbers just for the sake of crunching numbers. While hitting the targets in your budget each month is a good thing, it'll be more motivating and satisfying to make that a means to a greater end, such as pursuing a goal that matters to you.

Now think about a person in the top right quadrant. They have goals but no plan. What are they doing? They're *dreaming.* They have a destination in mind but no plan for getting there.

> [Alice] went on, "Would you tell me, please, which way
> I ought to walk from here?"
> "That depends a good deal on where you want to get to,"
> said the Cat.
> "I don't much care where—" said Alice.
> "Then it doesn't matter which way you walk," said the Cat.
> "—so long as I get somewhere," Alice added as an explanation.
> "Oh, you're sure to do that," said the Cat, "if you only
> walk long enough."
>
> **LEWIS CARROLL,** *ALICE IN WONDERLAND*

Last, look at the top left quadrant, where a person has some financial goals *and* a plan. This person is proactively *managing* money. That's exactly what a cash-flow plan enables you to do.

Putting the Plan into Action

There are three key steps to using a cash-flow plan.

1. Planning

Income is the starting point of budgeting. Once you know how much money is flowing into your life, you simply allocate portions of your income to each outgo category.

Before getting too detailed with these categories, let's consider the big five: spending, making debt payments, saving, investing, and giving. Those are the five actions you can take with money once you have some. And that's the order our consumer culture encourages.

In countless ways, the culture says, "Great! You're making seventy-five thousand dollars per year. That means you can drive this type of car, live in that type of neighborhood, and take this type of vacation." It's all about the spending. And when spending comes first, debt always comes along for the ride. (In fact, it *pays* for the ride!) After all that spending and all those debt payments, if there's anything left over, some might be saved or invested. And if anything is left over at *that* point, some might even be given away. But usually, there isn't much left over.

That framework—where spending comes first—helps explain why so many people have so much debt; find it so difficult to save, invest, and give; and experience so much financial stress.

Fortunately, there's a better way—a more biblical way. It looks like this: First, give a portion of all that you receive, then save and invest portions, and *then* see how much you can spend on a home, groceries, clothing, and all the rest. Along the way, avoid debt, with the possible exception of a reasonable mortgage.

More specifically, maybe you've heard of *10-10-80*. The idea is to give 10 percent, save and invest 10 percent, and then spend 80 percent. That's a fine approach, although I prefer *10-15-75*, especially if you hope to help your kids pay for college.

That framework—where giving, saving, and investing come before spending—is super simple and incredibly effective. If you set your priorities that way, your financial life will work amazingly well. And if you teach it to your kids, *their* financial lives will also work amazingly well.

To develop your own plan, first recognize that there's no such thing as a one-size-fits-all cash-flow plan. Everyone's situation is unique. The cost of living in a big city is very different than in a small town. Some people have access to heavily subsidized health insurance, and some don't. Tax rates and other costs vary, and so on. Still, there are certain principles for tackling this task that pertain to everyone. Here's how to go about developing your own plan.

Make generosity your first outgo category. As we'll discuss in the next chapter, that's what the Bible encourages when it teaches a "firstfruits" approach to generosity. A good starting point is to set giving at 10 percent of your gross income.

Next, allocate 10 to 15 percent to saving and investing. These are really two different categories, but they work hand in hand. If you don't have an emergency fund with three to six months' worth of essential living expenses, I recommend devoting the full amount to building one, although there are some caveats if you have any debts other than a reasonable mortgage. (We'll cover saving, investing, and debt in detail in chapters 6, 7, and 9.) For now, decide what percentage of gross income you will devote to the combined saving and investing category and enter that amount on your cash-flow plan. Also, list each of your monthly debt payments.

After filling in the giving, saving and investing, and debt sections on your cash-flow plan, move on to the various spending categories. Think of them as either essential or discretionary. Start with some of your more expensive essential categories, such as income taxes, housing, and health insurance. Then move on to transportation, food, and the more discretionary spending categories, such as clothing, entertainment, and vacations.

You may want to customize some of the categories. Early in our marriage, Jude and I had a shared clothing budget. We soon realized that this didn't work very well, so we created separate clothing budgets. Similarly, when our three children were young, we had a single "kids' clothing" budget. Today, those are three separate budgets, so now we have five clothing budgets!

Ultimately, you want your cash-flow plan to balance. (On my website, mattaboutmoney.com, you'll find sample cash-flow plans for households with various levels of income.) That means income minus outgo equals zero. While some categories are especially difficult to standardize, I recommend creating your cash-flow plan by starting with giving, saving, and investing. Many people struggle to find the money for these priorities because they hope money somehow will be "left over" for these purposes. Far better to make them your first priorities. Then enter your essential expenses and then your discretionary expenses.

If you find it difficult to balance your budget, we'll take a closer look at each of the most common spending categories in chapter 8. Don't worry—it won't be about obsessive frugality. It'll be about spending smart so you have enough for your priorities and you can spend with peace of mind. It'll be about determining what matters to you and allocating money accordingly. Maybe you value vacations more than wearing the latest fashions, so you allocate less to clothing and more to travel. That's one of the most beneficial aspects of using a cash-flow plan. Each category is like a lever that you can push or pull based on what's most important.

2. Tracking

This is the part of budgeting people usually dislike the most. However, electronic budgeting tools, like Mint, make the job much easier.

Once you link Mint or some other budgeting tool to your checking account and credit cards, it will automatically capture all your electronic spending and can even categorize your transactions. The only manual entries you have to make are for cash transactions.

It used to be that when I introduced the topic of budgeting in workshops, I could feel the energy drain from the room. I would ask for a show of hands as to how many people liked the idea of using a budget—and hardly a hand would go up. Some people would look at me like I was crazy. These days, I ask people early in workshops whether they use a budget and still get relatively few hands. However, later on, I ask whether anyone uses Mint or a similar online tool, and I see quite a few more hands. Apparently, online budgeting tools have taken much of the pain out of budgeting, enough that it doesn't even seem like budgeting to a lot of people. That's a very good thing.

Of course, you don't have to use an online budgeting tool. You could use an electronic spreadsheet or a simple paper-and-pencil system. Both would require more manual entry, but you wouldn't have to worry about online security. You could also use the envelope system, where you fill envelopes each month with the amount of money you have budgeted for groceries, entertainment, clothing, and other categories (except those you pay online, like your mortgage). Then you spend out of those envelopes. It may seem like an old-fashioned system, but it works really well and is a great way to introduce kids to budgeting.

What's the best budget system for you? The best option is the one you will actually use!

IS IT SAFE?

In order to use an online budgeting tool, you have to connect it to your checking account and credit cards, which requires entering your username and password for each account. Mint encrypts all such information so that no one can steal it. Also, it's a read-only service. You can view information when you access your Mint account, but you can't move any money around, so in the unlikely event that a hacker gains access to your account, he won't be able to do any damage. If you use a different online budgeting tool, make sure it also uses encryption and operates on a read-only basis.

---

3. Reviewing/Adjusting

While you should check at the end of each month to see how your actual spending compared to your planned spending, check throughout the month as well. Here again, an online tool makes this job super easy. Within seconds, you can see where you are with your entertainment budget and how your grocery budget is looking. Checking in with your cash-flow plan regularly is the key to *managing to the number* in each category. I like that phrase. It conveys the real benefit of a budget: It doesn't just tell you *what* happened—it enables you to *make* things happen.

As you write out your grocery list, if it's halfway through the month and you see that you've spent more than half your grocery budget, that tells you to focus on the essentials. If you have more room in your budget, you could pick up a treat or two.

I can't stress strongly enough how important it is to check in with your budget throughout the month. If you're out running errands and you notice there's a sale going on at your favorite clothing store, before you go inside, check to see how you're doing with your clothing budget. That'll tell you whether it's okay to shop the sale, and if so, how much you can spend.

At the end of the month, do a more detailed analysis. If you've overspent in a certain category, either you need to be more proactive about managing that category or the original number was unrealistic.

Doing a better job of managing to the number might be about checking more often to see how you're doing in that category and then being more intentional about staying on track. For example, if you find that you've spent most of your entertainment budget halfway through the month, you could seek out free or less expensive options for the rest of the month, like going for bike rides or playing board games.

On the other hand, if you're doing a good job of checking in with your plan and are being proactive about trying to hit the number and you're still consistently overspending in that category, your planned spending amount probably isn't realistic. You'll need to increase the amount while decreasing the amount in some other category.

Raising the Next Generation of Cash-Flow Managers

As soon as your kids have any money flowing into their lives, teach them that being intentional about how they use money is part of what it means to be a good steward (or manager). We don't want to be reckless with God's resources. We want to plan how to best use them.

Every Dollar Gets a Job

Even when your kids are pretty young, there are two essential budgeting lessons they can learn. The first is how to allocate portions of every dollar they receive toward different priorities. Initially, focus on three of the five main outgo categories: giving, saving, and spending. Teach them to give the first portion, save the second portion, and use the rest for spending. That's a beginner's budget.

To make this easy, there are piggy banks and other containers on the market that have separate slots for these three categories. You could also use Mason jars or envelopes.

Earlier, we talked about the 10-10-80 framework: give 10 percent, save 10 percent, and spend 80 percent. As I mentioned, I prefer 10-15-75, but that's for us adults. For kids, I think something like 10-50-40 makes more sense. There are so many expenses kids don't have that they *will* have when they're older (a mortgage or rent payment, taxes, insurance, groceries, etc.), that if they get in the habit of spending 75 to 80 percent of all they receive right now, that'll be unsustainable later on. Plus, our kids have a huge opportunity to save, so let's encourage them to make the most of that opportunity.

When your kids are really young and are receiving a very small amount of money, 10-10-80 is fine. But as they start receiving more, make some adjustments. Move them to 10-20-70, and then to 10-30-60, and on from there.

If You Don't Have It, You Can't Spend It

The second essential budgeting lesson young kids can learn is the importance of living within their means. That may seem kind of silly since we're talking about 40 to 80 percent of small amounts of money. But keep in mind that habits established early will be magnified later. I see that clearly as I look back on my own life.

I started earning money when I was in grade school, and I enjoyed spending it. When I got older, all those pesky adult expenses, like rent and utilities and groceries, really rained on my spending parade—until I discovered credit cards. Once again, I could spend freely, all the while doing my best to ignore my growing debts.

Building those early habits of spending everything I made cost me a lot. For far too long, I missed out on the joy and impact of giving. For far too long, I missed out on the satisfaction of buying things with savings. Meanwhile, for far too long, I missed out on the multiplying power of compounding that I could have experienced had I started to invest earlier. Then, for far too long, I had to shovel lots of money to creditors as I dug my way out of debt.

So let your kids experience the excitement of using their own money to buy candy or stickers, but make sure they learn to adhere to limits. If they use up all their spending money and then see something else they want to buy, don't come to their rescue. Don't give them an advance on next week's allowance, and don't buy the item for them. Let them feel the pain of regret over having so quickly spent all that they had. Put on your gatekeeper hat and wear it well.

Save Some for Later

The next time they receive some money, maybe (with a gentle reminder from you) they'll think more intentionally about how to use their spending money. As you get set to take them to the store, maybe they'll decide to leave some of it at home. Sometimes, maybe they'll decide to leave it *all* at home so they'll have more to spend on something more expensive later.

As they get older and receive more money, teach them to put their spending money into different envelopes for different purposes. Maybe some is for candy and some is for books. As they do this, the line between spending and saving may start to blur. If they hold onto some of their spending allocation for several weeks, is it still *spending* money, or is it savings? Great question. Let's call it future spending money.

When your kids begin choosing to hang on to more of their spending allocation for more expensive things they want to buy, they will be naturally transitioning themselves from 10-10-80 to 10-20-70 and beyond. This is a very good thing.

In chapter 8, I'm going to encourage you to eventually shift responsibility for certain spending categories, such as your kids' clothing, from you to them. At that point, using a budget will become a little more involved. Until then, developing these two skills—first, allocating any money they receive across the priorities of giving, saving, and spending; and second, living within their means—will get them started in the right direction. You can prepare them for more advanced budgeting lessons by bringing them into your household budgeting process.

Talking the Talk

Sometimes when I look at our online cash-flow plan, I'll tell any of our kids who happen to be nearby that I'm checking to see how our budgeting program has categorized some of our recent spending, making any changes that might be necessary, and taking a look at how we're doing compared to our plan.

When you talk about budgeting, choose your words carefully. Saying things like "Well, we sure blew the grocery budget last month" probably isn't going to make this whole money-management thing sound all that fun. If you did, in fact, overspend your grocery budget, it would be better to say something like, "Hmm, we seem to have spent more on groceries than planned. It's good to have a tool like this to let us know. We'll try to make up for it next month by focusing more on the essentials at the grocery store."

When John and Joan were raising their four children, they chose to be intentional about how they spoke to their kids. John said, "We tried not to say, 'We can't afford that.' That's just a really negative story to tell a child. It's an easy answer when they ask for something, but I think it imparts too many negative emotions. 'We couldn't afford this; we couldn't afford that.' How are those words going to play in their head later on?"

That's exactly what happened to Laura, whom we met earlier in this chapter. She had been so conditioned to believe that whatever she wanted wasn't affordable that she brought a fear of spending into her adulthood, even when she made enough money to afford more.

Instead of saying, "We can't afford it," John and Joan would say, "It's not in our plan right now" or "We'll save up for that."

That's another reason why it's so important to *have* a plan.

Opening the Books

When they're old enough (around age eight or so), it's important to include our kids in discussions about financial priorities so we can help them learn wise lessons about making trade-offs. For example, we're in the midst of planning a special trip that will take our annual vacation budget beyond where it's normally set. All three of our kids are on board with taking the money we would have spent on Christmas gifts and moving it to the vacation budget to help cover the cost.

Leo and Natalie have been even more open in talking with their kids about their household budget. They both came from families in which money was a source of much stress and strife, and early in their marriage they saw themselves repeating history. Natalie's enjoyment of giving gifts and Leo's preference for saving caused frequent conflicts. He felt that she was spending too much, and she thought he was being too controlling. A budget brought objectivity and flexibility to the table, allowing them to devote what they both agreed was enough money to each priority.

Using a budget was so helpful in getting Leo and Natalie onto the same financial page that they thought making their budget readily accessible to their two daughters might help get their whole family onto the same page. And it did.

"When they saw the budget, it stopped all the bickering and begging," Leo said. "'Why can't you buy me these hundred-dollar jeans?' We never had those arguments with them. We showed them: 'Here's the clothing budget.' They would say, 'It's back-to-school, so we need more to spend.' We would say, 'The clothing budget is what it is. You can save up over time if you want more for the fall.' Eventually they learned to handle it well."

In chapter 8, you'll meet a family who not only *showed* their daughter the family budget but actually had her *manage* it for a time before she left for college.

A Financial Power Tool

You don't have to share *all* the details of your family's finances with your kids, but if you don't use a budget, I strongly encourage you to start. I know you'll find it helpful in your own day-to-day money management, and it'll provide a great example for your kids.

Finally, keep in mind that budgeting isn't the goal. A budget is a means to an end. It's a tool that can help you and your kids live generously, save and invest adequately, and prioritize your spending. God has graciously appointed us as stewards over some of His resources. A cash-flow plan enables us to truly *manage* those resources.

Recap and Next Steps

A budget is the single most powerful tool anyone can use for managing money well. It will be a great help to you, and your positive experience with a budget will motivate your kids to use one. Contrary to popular opinion, a budget isn't something you *go on*, like a diet. A budget, or as I prefer to call it, a cash-flow plan, is a tool you use to proactively manage money in pursuit of your goals. There are three key steps: planning, tracking, and reviewing/adjusting. While there are various budgeting tools available and online budgeting tools have made the process easier than ever, the best one is the one you will actually use.

- The beginning of budgeting is getting your kids in the habit of allocating portions of every dollar they receive to giving, saving, and spending.

- Buy a piggy bank with three slots (one each for giving, saving, and spending) or use three Mason jars or three envelopes.

- At first, when your kids are receiving very little, 10-10-80 (giving 10 percent, saving 10 percent, and spending 80 percent) is a fine framework, but soon enough help them allocate more to saving and less to spending. Simply make them responsible for buying things that cost more.

- When your kids spend their own money, let them experience limits so they learn to live within their means. If they spend all they have but want something else, let them feel the pain of having to better plan how they will use any money they receive.

- Be careful how you talk about budgeting. Budgets get a bad enough rap already, so try not to talk about "blowing the budget," and avoid telling your kids you can't do something because you're on a budget. Help them see that a budget is a helpful tool for using money according to your priorities.

- Encourage your kids to memorize Proverbs 21:5: "The plans of the diligent certainly lead to profit, but anyone who is reckless certainly becomes poor" (HSCB).

CHAPTER 5

LIVING GENEROUSLY

The world of the generous gets larger and larger;
the world of the stingy gets smaller and smaller.
PROVERBS 11:24, MSG

ONE DAY, on a visit to Chicago from their suburban home, sixteen-year-old Will told his parents he had a quick errand to run. When he came back, he had twenty dollars' worth of McDonald's gift cards that he intended to give to some of the homeless people they kept encountering. He'd gotten the idea of giving restaurant gift cards instead of money from Mike Yankoski's *Under the Overpass*, which tells the story of America's homeless population via a couple of men who lived among them.

Will and his parents had been coming to Chicago frequently, but not to see the sights. Will was being treated for cancer. Remarkably, at a time when many people would have been drawing inward, Will was looking outward, noticing the needs of other people and doing what he could to help meet them. How does a young person develop such a generous heart? To explore that question, let's begin by looking at the big picture of biblical generosity. We'll return to Will's story soon.

Part of Our Design

Once, as our family headed out the door to welcome some new neighbors, gift basket in hand, I wasn't in a very good mood. I had a lot I wanted to get done that day and had forgotten to add this errand to my packed schedule. After ringing the doorbell, I did my best to put a smile on my face. By the time we returned home twenty minutes later, my mood had shifted completely. The other family's happiness over our small gesture was infectious, lifting my spirits considerably.

There's something very satisfying about contributing to the good of others. I guess that's why Jesus said, "It is more blessed to give than to receive" (Acts 20:35). In more recent years, countless secular studies have backed that up, demonstrating very clearly that generosity is an important part of a joyful life.

For example, in the book *Happy Money*, Elizabeth Dunn, associate professor of psychology at the University of British Columbia, and Michael Norton, associate professor of marketing at Harvard Business School, describe a study in which the spending habits of hundreds of Americans were analyzed. Dunn and Norton conclude, "The amount of money individuals devoted to themselves was unrelated to their overall happiness. What *did* predict happiness? The amount of money they gave away. The more they invested in others, the happier they were." And that was true no matter how much income people earned.[1]

God made us in His image. And because God is endlessly generous, that means generosity is woven into our spiritual DNA. When we're generous, we're expressing one of the most fundamental aspects of our nature and living in sync with our God-given design leads to a more fulfilling life.

Some people even trace material blessings to their generosity, an idea that may be affirmed in Proverbs 11:24-25: "One person gives freely, yet gains more; another withholds what is right, only to become poor. A generous person will be enriched, and the one who gives a drink of water will receive water" (HCSB).

Now, we need to be a bit careful here. I do not say this to encourage a *give-to-get* approach to giving. Popularized by the so-called prosperity gospel, giving *in order to get* something in return is not at all what the Bible teaches. As the apostle Paul asked, "Who has given a gift to [God] that he might be repaid?" (Romans 11:35). God is the Giver. Everything we have is a gift from Him.

Our giving is best done *because of* our gratitude for all that God has done for us and as an act of worship. If we benefit in any way from living generously—even if *just* by experiencing more happiness—that's just one more reason to continue down the path of generosity.

Your Heart Follows Your Wallet

One of the more interesting lessons the Bible teaches about generosity is that we don't need to wait for warm feelings of kindness to wash over us before acting generously toward others. The Bible says that our hearts will follow our wallets: "Where your treasure is, there your heart will be also" (Matthew 6:21).

When I first read that verse, I thought it made more sense the other way around—that our money will follow our hearts. We get excited about a certain car, and before we know it, we've spent our money to buy it. While things do work that way sometimes, biblical truth is both less intuitive and more powerful.

For a time, Jude and I provided some financial support for one of her friends, who was doing missionary work in Bolivia. Before then, I paid approximately zero attention to Bolivia. Honestly, I would have had a hard time quickly locating it on a map, and I certainly had no idea what was happening there. But when we started sending some money there, I took a lot of interest in each update my wife's friend sent us, and I began to notice every time Bolivia was in the news. My heart went there because some of our treasure was going there.

Money can have a strong hold over us. Giving it away breaks that hold. It redirects our thoughts from ourselves to others. Regularly investing in the people and issues that are on God's heart is a financial habit that can't help but deepen our relationship with Jesus.

Don't know where to start? Here is some practical, biblical guidance.

Put First Things First

Managing money well is largely about deciding what's most important. If our lifestyle is most important, which is what our consumer culture tells us, spending will come first, and debt will follow close behind. If our financial future is most important, which is what financial planners tell us ("pay yourself first"), saving will come first. But for wise builders, our relationship with Jesus is most important. That means investing in God's Kingdom work is our first financial priority: "Honor the LORD with your wealth and with the firstfruits of all your produce" (Proverbs 3:9).

Firstfruits refers to the first or best portion. *Produce* spoke to the agriculture-focused nature of so many people's livelihoods when the book of Proverbs was written. The King James Version of the Bible says to give "the firstfruits of all thine *increase*" (emphasis mine). I take that to mean we are to give back to God the first portion of any money that flows into our lives, no matter what the source.

Think Percentages

In both the Old and New Testaments, we see the principle of *proportionate* giving. Everyone was not instructed to give the same amount of money. People were instructed to give based on how much they'd received: "Every man shall give as he is able, according to the blessing of the LORD your God that he has given you" (Deuteronomy 16:17).

"On the first day of every week, each of you is to put something aside and store it up, as he may prosper, so that there will be no collecting when I come" (1 Corinthians 16:2). *As he may prosper. The Living Bible* translates this as "the amount [of your giving] depends on how much the Lord has helped you earn."

The Old Testament law described in Leviticus gets more specific: "Every tithe of the land, whether of the seed of the land or of the fruit of the trees, is the LORD's; it is holy to the LORD" (Leviticus 27:30). A *tithe* means "tenth part," or 10 percent.

In the New Testament, Jesus didn't abolish the standards of Old Testament law. He came to fulfill that law. But He made it clear that the Christian life isn't about mechanically following the letter of the law. He wants our hearts involved. Didn't kill anyone today? Well, *that's* good. But do you have anger in your heart? Didn't commit adultery today? I hope not! But did you look at anyone with impure thoughts? (See Matthew 5:17-30.)

Jesus applied that same standard—that our hearts must match our actions—to tithing:

> "Yes, woe upon you, Pharisees, and you other religious
> leaders—hypocrites! For you tithe down to the last mint
> leaf in your garden, but ignore the important things—
> justice and mercy and faith. Yes, you should tithe, but

you shouldn't leave the more important things undone."
(Matthew 23:23, TLB)

Giving 10 percent of our "increase" to Christ-centered purposes is the historical biblical starting point for the generous lives God designed us to live. And because the Bible speaks about tithes *and offerings*, tithing is clearly not His intended stopping point.

Partnering with Jesus

For help deciding where to give, here are some of the issues God cares about.

SPREADING THE GOSPEL

After Jesus' death and resurrection, His final instructions to His disciples were about telling others about Him:

> And Jesus came and said to them, "All authority in heaven and on earth has been given to me. Go therefore and make disciples of all nations, baptizing them in the name of the Father and of the Son and of the Holy Spirit, teaching them to observe all that I have commanded you. And behold, I am with you always, to the end of the age." (Matthew 28:18-20)

HELPING THE POOR

God's heart for the poor is written throughout the pages of Scripture, including in Proverbs 19:17: "Whoever is generous to the poor lends to the LORD, and he will repay him for his deed."

SUPPORTING THOSE WHO TEACH GOD'S WORD

Pastors and others involved in full-time ministry depend for their livelihood on the generosity of the people they serve. Therefore, "the one who is taught the word [of God] is to share all good things with his teacher [contributing to his spiritual and material support]" (Galatians 6:6, AMP).

The local church is a natural focal point for our giving because it is typically all about spreading the gospel, helping the poor, and teaching God's Word. Of course, there are many other issues God cares about as well, from disaster relief to helping persecuted Christians, from rescuing people from sex trafficking to strengthening marriages and more. We would be wise to be attentive to the ministries and individuals the Holy Spirit brings to our awareness and puts on our hearts.

> *I never would have been able to tithe the first million dollars I ever made if I had not tithed my first salary, which was $1.50 per week.*
>
> JOHN D. ROCKEFELLER

Raising the Next Generation of Generous Givers

The minute your children begin receiving money, whether from an allowance, a gift, or some other source, encourage them to give at least 10 percent to God. If your young kids are using a three-slotted piggy bank, keep it somewhere visible. Every time they receive money, teach them to put portions into each section right away, the first portion to God, the second portion for saving, and the third portion for spending. And, right from the beginning, be sure to teach them why.

While writing this book, I had coffee one morning with four young men, all in their twenties. All had been raised in Christian homes. All had seen their parents giving to their church. None of them understood why.

"I knew that my parents tithed," Matt said, "but it seemed like something they did just to check a box." Will agreed: "I remember seeing my parents giving, and they would give me a dollar to put in the offering. But as far as understanding *why* they were doing that, I don't know that I ever made a connection."

So help your kids understand that our generosity is a grateful response to God's generosity. He gave us everything we have. He gave us our very lives. He gave us His Son, Jesus. And He continues to give to us every day—the sunrise and the sunset, the roofs over our heads, the food on our tables. Giving is one very meaningful way to say thanks.[2]

In addition, there are a lot of needs in the world, and He invites us to come alongside Him in addressing those needs. When your kids give toward those needs, help them understand that they aren't giving to churches or ministries. They're giving directly to Jesus:

> "The King will say to those on his right, 'Come, you who are blessed by my Father, inherit the kingdom prepared for you from the foundation of the world. For I was hungry and you gave me food, I was thirsty and you gave me drink, I was a stranger and you welcomed me, I was naked and you clothed me, I was sick and you visited me, I was in prison and you came to me.' Then the righteous

will answer him, saying, 'Lord, when did we see you
hungry and feed you, or thirsty and give you drink? And
when did we see you a stranger and welcome you, or
naked and clothe you? And when did we see you sick or
in prison and visit you?' And the King will answer them,
'Truly, I say to you, as you did it to one of the least
of these my brothers, you did it to me.'" (Matthew
25:34-40)

It's important for our kids to see that the money they give is
impacting real people in real, life-changing, and even eternity-
shaping ways. The church that our family attends does a wonderful
job using videos to tell the stories of life change that God is bringing about through the initiatives and ministries we are all involved
in. Seeing those videos is encouraging, moving, and inspiring. It
helps us see that our giving is making a difference.

> *The life I touch for good or ill will touch another life,
> and in turn another, until who knows where the trembling
> stops or in what far place my touch will be felt.*
>
> FREDERICK BUECHNER, *THE HUNGERING DARK*

One of the ways we've tried to make our family's giving feel
real is by supporting several children through Compassion International. We know the names of the children, we have their
pictures, and we exchange letters with them. One evening over
dinner, we talked about Aziz, a young boy from Burkina Faso.
We sent him some extra money for his birthday, and he sent us a

picture in response, showing the extra rice and soap he bought for his family with the money.

The next morning, Jonathan, who was about six at the time, wandered into the kitchen rubbing the sleep out of his eyes. Being the loving father that I am, I hit him with a pop quiz about money: "Hey, Jonathan, do you remember the three things you can do with money?" He thought about it for a minute as he stretched his way through a big yawn and said, "You can spend it, you can save it, and, ah . . . you can give it to Aziz." I loved his answer!

Generosity as a Lifestyle

As I talk with other parents about how they've taught their kids about generosity, I hear again and again about the importance of getting kids involved with generosity as early as possible, even if that means giving just ten cents a week. It's also very important for our kids to see us giving regularly and hear us talking about it.

I heard about the importance of cultivating a bigger-picture view of others-centered living that is expressed in ways that go beyond giving money. For Dick and Sibyl, that meant having their boys share a bedroom, encouraging their kids to have something to contribute to the conversation at the dinner table, teaching them how to warmly welcome visitors into their home, having them participate in writing sympathy and get-well cards, and more.

Not far from where they raised their family in Cincinnati, there was a bus stop that served a poor community. When Dick and his sons noticed that the grass by the bus stop tended to get very overgrown and the area around it was littered with trash, they adopted the bus stop, regularly cutting the grass and picking up the trash.

"Yes, we taught the whole 'give some, save some, spend the rest' sort of thing," Dick said, "but I think the more important lessons were in how we lived."

That's a philosophy Keith and Cag were also intentional about living out when raising their four children: "I think they grew up seeing that it's important to have people in your home and to cook meals for people when they're sick," Cag said. "It's that sort of thing, regular acts of generosity, bit by little bit. They see that, and it becomes part of who they are."

Catching the Generosity Bug

Now let's pick up Will's story, which I introduced earlier in this chapter. Will's parents, John and Joan, are hesitant to take credit for growing Will's generous spirit. But Will understood his parents' stories and how they discovered the blessings of giving generously. John admits that early in his marriage he hadn't been the most generous guy on the block. He would put five or ten dollars into the weekly offering, even after beginning his career in a lucrative field. While Joan had been a committed Christ follower, John's faith was marginal at best.

"I started out as a young engineer with only a passing involvement with church, well on my way to becoming another statistic of American consumerism—and another rich young ruler," John says, referencing the conversation between Jesus and a wealthy young man described in Mark 10:17-27.

John and Joan were both savers, products of parents who had necessarily placed a high value on frugality. "They clung tightly to what they had, and they didn't have much," Joan said of her parents, who both grew up during the Great Depression. "As a farm family, you don't know how things are going to be. We didn't go on vacation, didn't go out to eat. My parents saved everything.

They cut open the toothpaste tube, straightened used nails, and scraped out the mayo jar."

Making generosity a priority in their family was Joan's idea. She knew from a young age that the tight hold her parents had on money—and that money had on them—was a habit she wanted to break. Her study of Scripture gave her a desire to tithe, a concept that hadn't ever even occurred to John.

John's faith was strengthened through the couple's involvement in a church in suburban Chicago. At one weekend service, a Haitian missionary talked about the hardship faced by the many homeless families in the Caribbean. John had three thousand dollars of savings earmarked for a new set of stereo speakers, but when he heard that this amount could provide an entire home for a family, he decided to give it all away. He never did replace those speakers.

Before long, he got involved in their church's stewardship ministry, Good $ense, and got to know its director, Dick Towner, my friend and longtime mentor. John says, "Under Dick's teaching, I found out that God owns it all and I need to be a steward of all He provides."

John was also moved by the idea of having a financial finish line that would help him and Joan decide how much is enough. "It's such a treadmill the other way," he realized. "As soon as you take two steps, you see the next two steps you want to take. Unless you have a goal and know the finish line, you're going to be miserable."

That idea helped him and his wife resist the temptation to trade up to a bigger home or nicer car each time their income increased. It gave them margin and peace of mind, enabling Joan to be home with their growing family, and it fueled their increasing passion for generosity—for letting go of more and more of what God had entrusted to them.

One year, when their church was in the midst of a building campaign, John felt prompted to give 10 percent of their entire net worth.

"I was surprised at the number, especially since it was coming from John," Joan said. "I was praying for many years that he would become a Christian, and now here he was displaying phenomenal generosity." She was completely on board with the gift.

As the years passed and their kids grew older, living others-centered lives became a deeply entrenched core value in their family. John and Joan's conviction to hold the things of this world with a loose grip strongly informed their parenting. They became very intentional about fostering this worldview within Will and their other three children.

Life Interrupted

One summer day, in the midst of preparations for a family vacation, John and Joan decided to take Will to the doctor. It was just a precaution. The athletic teen had been feeling unusually lethargic, and they thought he might have mono.

But it wasn't mono. It was cancer. Joan recalls trying to process the devastating news and wondering how to begin navigating this journey. She thought of one of their church's pastors, whose daughter was being treated for cancer, and called him.

"I asked him to think back to day one of their journey. 'What would you have wanted to know? What should we know?' And he said, 'That Will is God's son first.' I thought, *That's a pretty crummy answer. What else you got?* I thought I'd hear about a dream-team doctor or get some other practical advice. But there was something in those words that reminded me what faith really is, what trust really is. Those aren't just words. These kids aren't really ours. They're God's first."

Initially, Will's prognosis was fairly good. However, chemotherapy eventually exhausted his immune system. A year after his diagnosis, Will died from an infection.

"Little did I know that God would be asking us to let go of even more of what He had given us," Joan said.

At the hospital, John and Joan witnessed many families torn apart by the emotional and financial stress of their children's illnesses, but that was not their experience. While they felt all the emotions that go with such an unimaginable loss—deep sadness, anger, moments of doubt—they drew strength from God along the way. Their years of investing in their relationship with Him and their relationships with their family and community of friends saw them through the tragedy.

Through Will's death, John and Joan saw a whole new dimension of the value they had established as a family years earlier—to hold loosely the things of this world.

"When the greatest treasure you've been entrusted with is suddenly gone, you begin to understand more of what it means not to store up treasures on earth," Joan said. "We've learned through loss that everything on this side of heaven is temporary. Our perspective changed, our faith got painfully stretched, and our focus shifted quickly away from goals of achieving and acquiring more treasures. Our hands opened up."

Knowing a little bit about John and Joan's story, it's easier to understand why their son would have been looking outward in the midst of his cancer treatments, why he would have been so aware of other people's needs, and why he would have been so intent on helping meet those needs.

John and Joan continue to live others-centered lives. Both are heavily involved in ministry. And whenever they go into Chicago, they continue to do what they can to help the homeless people they encounter. They've maintained an ongoing friendship with one of them, Roger, whom they kept running into on their many trips to the city with Will.

Our stories may not be as dramatic as John and Joan's, but they can be just as impactful. It takes teaching our kids by word and deed about biblical generosity. Yes, let's teach them about firstfruits giving, about proportionate giving, and about tithes and offerings. But let's make sure they don't grow up thinking of generosity as a bill to be paid or a box to be checked. Let's raise our kids to live others-centered lives. Let's foster within them hearts that break for the world's great needs. And let's equip them to boldly and bravely partner with Jesus in helping meet those needs, whether that means serving in a third-world country thousands of miles away or joining the kid who's sitting all alone in the school cafeteria. An others-focused perspective will infuse their lives with great meaning and joy, and it will enrich their relationship with Jesus and others as nothing else can.

If your kids are very young, teaching them to put ten cents of every dollar into the giving slot of their piggy bank may seem like a small thing. However, the exponential returns God can generate through a life lived generously will go on and on, impacting your children's lives—and the lives of others they touch with their compassion—in countless good ways.

Recap and Next Steps

We were made in God's image, and God is endlessly generous. This means that we were designed to live generously. The Bible gives us some guidelines here. It says to make generosity our first financial priority and to give proportionately. This means that not everyone is expected to give the same amount but rather a percentage of our "increase" (any money that flows into our lives). The biblical starting point is 10 percent. As for where to give, some of the purposes God clearly cares about include spreading the gospel, helping the poor, and supporting those who teach God's Word. Since the local church is about all three of those purposes, that's a natural starting point and focal point for our generosity. God will also put other ministries or individuals on our hearts to support. Regularly investing in God's purposes is one of the most satisfying things we can do with money. By fostering hearts of generosity in our kids, we will set them up for a lifetime of using money with meaning and joy.

- The minute your kids receive their first dollar, encourage them to give 10 percent of it to God.

- Be sure to explain the purposes of generosity. It's a way of thanking God for all that He does for us, and it's a deeply satisfying experience to partner with Him in helping meet some of the many needs in the world.

- Make giving real for your kids. Put a face to their generosity by helping them know whom they are impacting. Sponsoring a child through an organization like World Vision or Compassion International can help.

- Teach your children that, ultimately, when they give to help meet a need in Jesus' name, they are giving directly to Jesus.

- Show your kids that generosity is a lifestyle. Yes, it's about giving money. But it's also about bringing meals to people who are sick, having something to contribute to the conversation during dinner, and sitting with a kid who's all alone in the cafeteria.

- Encourage your kids to memorize Proverbs 11:24. It's paraphrased in *The Message* this way: "The world of the generous gets larger and larger; the world of the stingy gets smaller and smaller."

CHAPTER 6

SAVING PATIENTLY

The wise man saves for the future,
but the foolish man spends whatever he gets.
PROVERBS 21:20, TLB

PEOPLE SOMETIMES ASK ME what makes biblical money management, well, biblical. Some of the financial principles found in Scripture are so practical that they can seem like nothing more than common sense. Consider the proverb above. It seems obvious that it's wise to save and foolish to spend whatever we get! What's so uniquely biblical about that? The story of two young sisters provides a good answer.

As soon as they became aware of money, Rachel and Courtney (daughters of Leo and Natalie, whom we met in chapters 3 and 4), were taught the importance of generosity as a first financial priority and saving as a second priority. Giving the first portion of whatever they'd received and saving the second portion were habits they developed early in their lives. One year, when they were just three and five years old, they desperately wanted a trampoline, so their parents gave them a list of chores they could do to earn money, and they went to work.

Just when they had earned almost enough for the trampoline they wanted so badly, the girls heard a missionary speak at their church. They were so moved by the work he was doing that they decided to support him with a sizable portion of the money they had saved.

Soon after, their aunt got in touch with them. She knew that the girls had been saving for a trampoline, but she had no idea they had given away a large portion of their savings. She called to report that the store where she worked had a trampoline on clearance. In addition, she could use her employee discount to lower the price further. That enabled the girls to buy the trampoline with the money they had left over after their gift to the missionary.

"That was such a God thing," Leo said. "It was a great lesson that showed them how generosity works."

It was an example of what my mentor, Dick Towner, likes to call "God's math." Yes, the biblical teaching to save for the future is the same as what secular money-management teachers recommend. But holding savings loosely—with an open hand and a willingness to use them for purposes outside our plans as the Holy Spirit prompts us to—is uniquely biblical. As God beautifully taught Rachel and Courtney at a young age, managing money this way often leads to unexpected blessings.

Three Types of Savings

When I was spending my way into debt, I made pretty much every mistake possible, including not putting money into savings. And if I had any savings, I'm sure I wouldn't have been very open to giving them away!

While my saving habits may have been worse than most people's, many of us are not exactly saving superstars. About one-third of adults in the US say they would not be able to come up with two thousand dollars within the next month if an unexpected need arose. Almost half have less than three months' worth of living expenses in savings.[1]

Without money in reserve, when things go wrong, the only option is to go into debt. Having money in savings helps us avoid debt and greatly reduces stress, which is a far more enjoyable way to live. Here are three essential types of savings for all of us adults.

1. An Emergency Fund

In life, stuff goes wrong—often at the worst possible time. And yet, too many of us have too little set aside for those situations. What about you? How easily could you come up with two thousand dollars in the next thirty days? Building an emergency fund is the first step in a solid saving strategy.

Ideally, you would have 10 to 15 percent of monthly gross income flowing into the combined saving and investing category. If you don't have an emergency fund, use that full amount to build that fund first.

If you have any debt other than a reasonable mortgage, build an emergency fund that totals one month's worth of essential expenses. Then take that 10 to 15 percent of monthly gross income and redirect it toward making accelerated payments on your debts. Once they are paid off, redirect it back to savings and build a larger emergency fund.

Ultimately, your emergency fund should total three to six months' worth of essential monthly expenses. Look at your cash-flow plan and figure out what one month's worth of essential expenses amounts to for your household. If you lost your job tomorrow, you wouldn't need to spend money on clothing, entertainment, or vacations, but you *would* need to cover your mortgage or rent, utilities, all your different insurance payments, food, gasoline, and any debt payments. Take that monthly total and multiply it by three. Then multiply the monthly total by six. Those two numbers represent the range you're aiming for.

So which is it? Three months' worth of essential expenses or six? It depends on how many "breakable" moving parts you have in your life. If you have one child, rent an apartment, have a solid job situation—either your job seems secure or you have work skills that are in demand—and have reliable transportation, you may be okay with three months' worth of essential expenses in your emergency fund. But if you have more than one child, own your own home, have a shakier job situation, and your car isn't in such great shape, it would be best to build a bigger reserve.

Once you have enough in an emergency fund, you can take a large portion of what you have been saving and redirect it toward investing, but not all of it. Continue setting aside some money for the next savings priority.

2. A Big-Ticket-Item Replacement Fund

Think about the expensive things in your life that will eventually need to be replaced. How old are your furnace and air conditioner? What about your roof? When do you plan to replace your car?

Once your emergency fund is fully stocked, start putting money into a big-ticket fund. If you've been putting 12 percent of your income into the emergency fund, you could take most of that amount (say 10 percent of your gross income) and reallocate it to investing while continuing to save 2 percent for the big-ticket fund.

If you have to pay for a big-ticket item earlier than planned, you'll have to use your emergency fund. If this happens, be sure to start replenishing it as soon as possible, even if that means temporarily pausing contributions to your retirement account.

3. A Periodic-Bills-and-Expenses Fund

Some expenses occur every week or month, such as your mortgage or rent payment, groceries, gasoline, entertainment, utility bills, and health insurance. Others occur less frequently, such as property taxes (if you pay them separately from your mortgage); homeowner's, auto, and life insurance; vacations; and Christmas gifts. For these periodic bills and expenses, figure out each one's annual cost, add them all up, divide by twelve, and transfer that money into savings each month.

This doesn't require a separate allocation of income beyond the amount you've allocated to saving and investing. It just requires making sure your cash-flow plan accounts for the monthly cost of all periodic bills and expenses, and then, because you're not spending the money every month, transferring it into savings and keeping it there until the bill needs to be paid.

Let's say vehicle insurance costs you six hundred dollars every six months and you have budgeted $750 for Christmas gifts this year. So your cash-flow plan should have a vehicle insurance category with one hundred dollars per month allocated to it and a Christmas gifts category at $62.50. Every month you would transfer those amounts into savings.

It's important to have all such expenses listed on your cash-flow plan. That way, you will have accounted for expenses you'll have to pay at *some* point, so the money will be spoken for. But don't just let this money build up in your checking account. Mingled money leaks. You might start to believe you have extra funds for other spending categories. Transfer the money to savings each month and earmark it for these periodic bills and expenses.

Take a minute now to go through your cash-flow plan and determine which expenses don't need to be paid every month but *do* need to be paid at some point in the year. Figure out the total of all such periodic bills and expenses and then start transferring that amount into savings each month. This will smooth out your cash flow and dial down the stress that periodic expenses can cause.

Where to Keep Your Savings

Credit unions or online banks are good choices for the above types of savings because they usually pay higher interest rates than traditional brick-and-mortar banks. Some online banks allow you to set up multiple savings accounts you can name individually. That can be really helpful. When you log in, you can see exactly how much you have in your emergency fund, your car replacement fund, your Christmas gifts fund, and all the rest. Or you could have one big periodic-bills-and-expenses savings account. If so, just be sure to maintain a spreadsheet that specifies how much of that lump sum is earmarked for each category.

I'm guessing you'll agree that it would be wise to maintain the three types of savings we just discussed. Doing so probably seems logical. At the same time, we would be wise to remember the example of Rachel and Courtney and be attentive to the leadings of God, should He have other plans for the money we set aside.

Raising the Next Generation of Savers

When our kids are very young, the starting point in teaching them to be good savers is simply establishing saving as an expectation.

Just as with giving, the minute your kids have any money flowing into their lives, get them in the habit of saving a portion of every dollar.

Using a piggy bank with three sections—one for giving, one for saving, and one for spending—will provide a good visual cue that will instill in them a mindset that saving a portion of every dollar they receive is right and good and normal.

How Much to Save

In the planning chapter, we talked about the 10-10-80 framework (give 10 percent, save 10 percent, spend 80 percent). I said that this is fine for adults, although I prefer 10-15-75. For kids, though, I think something like 10-50-40 makes more sense.

What to Save For

As soon as possible, help your children experience the satisfaction of saving by having them save for something that doesn't take very long to save for. Maybe a book or an inexpensive toy—something they couldn't afford on the saving portion of this week's allowance or earnings alone, but could if they saved for two or three weeks.

As they get older, encourage each of them to save for more expensive things that take longer to save for, like a skateboard or a bike. As the items they want get more expensive, it'll be necessary for them to save more than 10 percent of every dollar they receive, so it will probably feel like a natural progression for them to save a higher percentage of whatever they receive. But feel free to help them connect the dots: "If you don't use all your spending money at the grocery store, you'll have more for the new LEGO set you want."

Where to Save

Eventually, move your kids from a piggy bank to a real bank. When we lived in the Chicago area, we opened savings accounts for each of our kids at a wonderful local bank. It had a small, movable staircase that could be positioned in front of a teller window. Each kid would step up, greet the teller, hand over their passbook, and give the teller the money they wanted to put into their account, usually in coins. The teller would record the deposit in the passbook and hand it back, showing them the amount that was being deposited, how much interest they'd earned, and their current balance. I loved how tangible it was. Especially for young kids, for as long as it's still possible, have them handle cash and coins.

Even though your kids won't earn much interest when they get started with saving, it will introduce them to an important new idea and a new reward for saving. Eventually, in pursuit of a better interest rate, switch them to an online bank. Just be sure to take them for a "visit" at least once a month to see their starting balance, any deposits made, how much they've earned in interest, and their current balance.

Reasons to Save

The habit of saving money provides benefits to our kids that go beyond being able to buy more expensive things and earning interest.

IT INTRODUCES THEM TO THE REAL WORLD

Soon enough, our kids will discover that every day isn't their birthday. People won't just give them things. They'll have to work and save for what they want. The sooner they understand this truth, the better. You may be in a position to buy your kids a lot of what they want, but it'll be good for them to have to save for some of it. It'll help prevent them from feeling entitled.

> *Good parents often do too much for their children.*
> *This is their one great mistake.*
>
> DR. EDWARD HALLOWELL, *THE CHILDHOOD ROOTS OF ADULT HAPPINESS*

IT HELPS THEM VALUE WHAT THEY BUY

It's human nature to appreciate something we worked for and spent our own money on more than something that was given to us. Our kids will find it satisfying to buy something with money they've earned and saved for over time, and having done so will motivate them to take good care of what they buy.

IT GIVES THEM OPTIONS

Our kids may not experience the same type of financial emergencies we experience, but then again, if we let them (and we should), they just might. When one of our boys was ten years old, he knocked a glass of water onto a laptop computer that led to an expensive repair. We made him pay for half. That required pretty much draining his savings, and it put an end to his allowance a year earlier than planned.

A tough lesson? Absolutely. Too harsh on our part? I don't think so. He was swinging a large cardboard tube in the kitchen, and we'd asked him more than once to stop. Having to take some responsibility for a costly problem he caused introduced him to reality.

When Dick and Sibyl's boys accidentally broke a glass display case at their school, they had to pay for half of that as well. "We decided that when they got in trouble, we would go in fifty-fifty," Sibyl explained. "Our idea was that there isn't any place where Christ does not go, where His grace does not go. Sometimes, when a kid has broken or lost something expensive, it's way too much for them at that time. It undoes them. It's too overwhelming. So we wanted to be parents who go fifty-fifty."

A wonderful other option that savings creates relates to generosity, as we saw with the story of Rachel and Courtney at the beginning of this chapter. I know of several other kids who had been dutifully saving for something only to hear about a need and feel prompted to give away some or all of their savings.

I've often thought that debt can make it hard to hear God's voice. Having too many bills to pay can make a prompting to give toward a particular need seem impossible. As Rachel and Courtney's story demonstrates so well, the opposite is also true. Having money in reserve can enable us to not just sense God's promptings but also to respond. Experiencing this at a young age could help children develop a uniquely powerful, God-glorifying view of money.

Here, too, we might be tempted to interfere: "Aw, honey, that's really sweet, but you don't need to give away the money you were saving for a new doll." Let's not rob our kids of the joy of Spirit-led giving, and let's not get in the way of a blessing God may have in store for them.

The Rewards of Waiting

There's one more important benefit to teaching our kids to save: It fosters the development of a uniquely powerful character trait— the ability to delay gratification.

You may have heard of the "Marshmallow Test." That's the common name for an experiment psychologist Walter Mischel conducted in the late 1960s and early 1970s at Stanford University. Mischel and his assistants tested hundreds of preschoolers to see how long they could hold out against the temptation of an immediate reward and wait for a bigger reward.

One at a time, the children were brought into a room by a researcher where they were given their choice of treats, including marshmallows. They were told that the researcher had to leave the room to do some work. If the child wanted to eat one treat, all they had to do was ring a bell. That would signal the researcher to return, and the child could have the treat. If instead the child could wait for the researcher to return on their own, they could have two treats. They weren't told how long the researcher would be gone, but it turned out to be about twenty minutes.

Some of the children could hardly wait at all. Pretty much the minute the researcher left, they rang the bell. But some found ways to wait the full twenty minutes and got to enjoy the greater reward.

Ten years later, Mischel checked in on the children, asking their parents and teachers to rate the kids, now adolescents, on a variety of traits. There were clear differences between the kids who'd been able to wait and those who hadn't. The "high delay" kids not only continued to exhibit strong self-control, but they were also rated more highly on concentration, attentiveness, self-reliance, confidence, stress management, planning, organization, perseverance, and goal accomplishment. Those who had been able to wait even did better on their college entrance exams, with the kids in the top third on the Marshmallow Test scoring an average of 210 points higher on the SAT than those in the bottom third.[2]

Another ten years later, Mischel followed up again, and

differences continued to be evident. The high-delayers were found to be more resilient, better at maintaining close relationships, and more successful at accomplishing long-term goals. They had attained higher levels of education and were even in better health. In fact, each additional minute that a preschooler delayed gratification ended up predicting a 0.2-point reduction in body mass index in adulthood.[3]

Think about all that the next time your five-year-old pushes back on the idea of saving a portion of his allowance!

Nature vs. Nurture

If you're worried that your kids aren't good at waiting, Mischel is convinced that the ability to delay gratification can be taught. While some of it is prewired, he says, "much of it remains open to learning."[4]

Mischel chose preschoolers for the Marshmallow Test because age four was the youngest age he found that children can begin to grasp the idea that choosing one treat now means missing out on two treats later.[5] But it isn't as if a switch suddenly gets flipped at that age. That's just when some can start to understand the trade-off and choose strategies that will help them wait. While this ability develops faster in some kids than others, Mischel says that all kids can get better at waiting.

Here are the mechanics of waiting and some ideas for helping our kids put this skill to use in saving for something they want to buy.

THEY HAVE TO WANT TO WAIT

For some kids, the willingness to wait will develop through the experience of spending this week's whole allowance, seeing something else they want, and realizing that they're out of money. It's important to let them feel the pain of regret and not give an advance on next week's allowance or buy them that next item.

For others, clarity and excitement about a future goal will motivate them to wait. We can help by asking them what they would like to buy, encouraging them to find out the cost, and then teaching them to break it down to weekly or monthly savings goals.

THEY HAVE TO KNOW HOW TO MAKE WAITING EASIER

There are two fundamental lessons Mischel took from the Marshmallow Test. First, the children who were the most successful at waiting were the ones who understood what they could do to overcome temptation. He saw some kids who initially couldn't wait a minute learn to wait for twenty when they changed their thoughts about the temptations. Second, we parents can help our children become better at waiting.

There are a couple of strategies to do this. This first is to "cool it." In the Marshmallow Test, the kids who could wait used a variety of strategies to turn the temperature down on the tempting treat in front of them. For some, that simply meant not looking at it. They closed their eyes or turned away.

For younger kids whose weekly spending money always seems to burn a hole in their pockets, this might mean not taking them to the store where they will be tempted to spend. Or it could mean closing the Bank of Mom and Dad. If we require them to save for some of the things they want, eventually they should stop thinking of us as their personal ATMs. For older kids who have their own email addresses, removing temptation could be about staying off the email lists of favorite brands.

Even more powerfully, pair the removal of temptations with

the addition of an image of what they're saving for. If a child is having a difficult time saving for a skateboard, reduce their exposure to other things they're tempted to spend their money on *and* put a picture of the skateboard they want in their room.

One more way to put a temptation on ice is to add a waiting period to a potential purchase. When any of John and Joan's kids mentioned something they wanted, they had to write it down and then wait two weeks before they could buy it. Oftentimes, their kids ended up not wanting the item after all. Writing it down and having to wait a while cooled the temptation that felt so strong in the moment.

Another strategy Mischel encourages is helping kids "time shift" their perspective from *now* to *later*. I like how parent and blogger Nikki Cox does this with her kids:

> After coming in from playing outside in the snow I watched them fling their wet stuff everywhere, leaving their boots and coats in various places. Having been through this before I know how this is going to end. When we want to leave to go somewhere or go play outside again the kids would be frustrated and unable to find their things, which in turn would cause me to become frustrated too.
>
> I stopped the kids and said, "Let's think of future us." Let's hang up all our wet clothing so it's dry when we want to go out and play again and not stinky and wet. Let's put our boots away in their cubby so we know right where to find them later and we don't get frustrated.
>
> To my complete and total surprise, the kids were like, yes. Let's do that. That makes sense.[6]

It's a strategy Cox uses on herself as well. "Go to bed early and get rest or stay up late? Let's think of future us. Spend money now on unnecessary stuff to clutter our home or save for intentional purchases or experiences in the future? Let's think of future us."[7]

When your son is tempted to spend more than planned at the toy store, encourage him to "think of future you." More specifically, have him think about how satisfying it will be to get something else he's been saving for.

THEY HAVE TO SEE PROGRESS

Kids need to see themselves getting closer to their goals. A visual indicator can help. We've all seen the huge thermometers that towns set up when a philanthropic group is raising money for a good cause. If your daughter is saving for some new field hockey gear, have her put a picture of it in her room and then either draw or print a picture of a thermometer, write the savings goal at the top, and then have her color it in as she makes progress.

THEY HAVE TO CROSS THE FINISH LINE

Walter Mischel said, "There's no good reason for anyone to forgo the 'now' unless there is trust that the 'later' will materialize."[8] So we have to make sure our kids experience the satisfaction of accomplishing their goals. Especially when they accomplish goals that have taken a long time and required saving a lot of money, be sure to celebrate their achievements.

FINANCIAL BENEFITS AND MORE

Helping our kids learn how to set goals to save for things they want to buy, use strategies to overcome the many temptations that could take them off course, track their progress, and see their goal through to completion will benefit them financially and in many other ways. Mischel says that such skills give children "a powerful advantage that can help them succeed and maximize their potential throughout their lives."[9]

But let's also remember what makes the practical advice to save for the future biblical. Let's hold savings with an open hand and use them as God directs, and let's encourage our kids to do the same.

Recap and Next Steps

Building and maintaining savings is a foundational part of good stewardship. It'll help us avoid debt and stress. Save for three purposes: emergencies, the replacement of big-ticket items, and periodic bills and expenses. Keep all such savings separate from your checking account. As we help our kids cultivate the habit of saving, keep in mind that we are helping them develop one of the most important character traits there is—the ability to delay gratification.

- As soon as your kids have any money flowing into their lives, get them in the habit of saving a portion of it.

- If your kids use up all their spending money and then see something else they want to buy, your response will make a big difference in whether they learn to save or not. Just say no to an advance on next week's allowance.

- Over time, give your kids responsibility for buying more expensive things, which should naturally move them toward saving a higher percentage of any money they receive.

- Help your kids progress from saving in a piggy bank to saving at a local bank or credit union to saving at an online bank.

- If your kids break or lose something expensive, don't be afraid to have them cover at least half the cost, even if that means using up much or all of their savings. That'll help them experience the real world. By the same token, if they see a need and feel prompted to give away some or all of their savings, let them experience the joy of doing so.

- Teach your kids the "cool it" and "time shift" strategies to help them wait as they save for something that will take some time, and make sure they experience the rewards of waiting.

- Encourage your kids to memorize Proverbs 21:20: "The wise man saves for the future, but the foolish man spends whatever he gets" (TLB).

CHAPTER 7

MULTIPLYING MONEY

Steady plodding brings prosperity;
hasty speculation brings poverty.
PROVERBS 21:5, TLB

WHAT IF OUR KIDS could have their retirements largely funded by the time they finished high school? A crazy idea? Unrealistic? I don't think so.

If our children can save three thousand dollars by the time they are eighteen years old and invest that money wisely, it can very realistically grow to well over a million dollars by the time they're seventy, even if they never invest another penny. That's far more than most people end up with *after working for an entire lifetime*! And if our kids hold the money in a Roth IRA, it'll all be tax-free.

Where will the three thousand dollars come from? If our kids get some cash for their birthdays or Christmas, or if they start doing some jobs for money between ages ten and fourteen (dog walking, babysitting, mowing lawns, a paper route), and if they get more of a *real* part-time job when they're fourteen to eighteen (working at a restaurant, a golf course, a retailer), saving three thousand dollars by age eighteen should be very doable.

The prospect of turning three thousand dollars at age eighteen into over a million dollars by age seventy shows what's possible if our kids take full advantage of their most valuable asset: time.

There's nothing magical about three thousand dollars or age eighteen. The point is simply that starting to invest at a young age can be very beneficial. I'll give more specifics about this idea in a few minutes. First, let's talk about ways that we adults can invest well.

Investing Essentials

The Bible tells us it's good stewardship to multiply money. In the parable of the talents, the two servants who double what their master entrusted to them are strongly affirmed. The one who doesn't do anything productive with what he received is strongly rebuked.

But motives matter. We don't want to be like the wealthy guy Jesus called out in Luke 12:16-21. He had accumulated plenty but had become preoccupied with building new barns to store his surplus, and he began daydreaming about a life of leisure. God called him a fool.

It can be wise to invest in order to help our kids pay for college or take care of our families in our later years. While our whole lives are to be about service and impact, most of us very likely will one day retire from full-time paid work. In fact, at some point many of us will *have to* retire because of our health, the health of a loved one, or a job loss. Preparing for such a day by building a nest egg to live on will help us fulfill the biblical mandate to provide for our families that we see in 1 Timothy 5:8: "If anyone does not provide for his relatives, and especially for members of his household, he has denied the faith and is worse than an unbeliever."

Here are the key ways we as parents can invest in the future of our families.

Make a Plan

Another translation of Proverbs 21:5 says, "The plans of the diligent certainly lead to profit, but anyone who is reckless certainly becomes poor" (HCSB). A good *investment* plan includes a *goal*, its estimated cost, when you'd like to accomplish it, and how much you will need to invest each month to get there. (At mattaboutmoney .com, you'll find recommended calculators to help you figure all that out for retirement and college-funding goals.)

For retirement, you'll also need to know your investing temperament. At the intersection of your time frame and your temperament is your optimal asset allocation—that is, the right mix of aggressive stock-based investments and more conservative bond-based investments. (You'll find links to free resources for determining that at my website as well.)

The stock market isn't the only place where you can invest. However, for a lot of us, it's the most accessible place. Perhaps your employer offers a 401(k) or 403(b) plan. If not, it's easy enough to open an individual retirement account (IRA) at a broker like Vanguard, Fidelity, or Charles Schwab.

As we talked about in a previous chapter, I recommend allocating 10 to 15 percent of monthly gross income to the combined saving-and-investing category, with a priority on building savings first. Once your emergency fund has three to six months' worth of essential living expenses (and your debts other than a reasonable mortgage are paid off), redirect most of that money to investing while you continue to save some of it for the replacement of big-ticket items.

Choose Your Account Type

For retirement, you'll want to pursue your goal through a tax-advantaged retirement account like a 401(k) and/or an IRA.[1] And you may have a choice between a traditional or a Roth 401(k) or IRA.

With a traditional account, the money you contribute is tax-deductible. If you earn eighty thousand dollars and contribute five thousand dollars to a traditional 401(k) or IRA, your taxable income for that year becomes seventy-five thousand dollars. In exchange for that immediate tax benefit, when you start withdrawing from your account in retirement, all the money you take out will be taxable. With a Roth, there is no immediate tax benefit. If you earn eighty thousand dollars and contribute five thousand dollars, your taxable income is still eighty thousand dollars. However, when you withdraw money in retirement, all of it will be tax-free. Generally, younger people who are not earning as much as they may earn later will benefit more from a Roth.

For college, using what's known as a *529 plan* (named after an IRS tax rule) will provide at least one tax benefit, and possibly two: First, investment gains are tax-free, as long as the money is used for college expenses, such as tuition and room and board. Second, some states provide a state income tax deduction or credit for contributions. Search on the name of your state and "529 plan" to find more details.

Choose Your Investments

When considering what to invest in, use mutual funds instead of individual stocks because mutual funds are inherently diversified, which is a principle promoted in Scripture: "Divide your investments among many places, for you do not know what risks might lie ahead" (Ecclesiastes 11:2, NLT). When you buy even a single share of a mutual fund, your money is divided across many stocks, bonds, or other investments.

As for which funds to invest in, here are four ways to approach investing, each of which will point you to appropriate investments.

1. DO IT YOURSELF

To go it alone with your investing, figure out your optimal asset allocation, and then use a small number of index funds to invest accordingly. For example, to build a portfolio with 90 percent stocks and 10 percent bonds, you could build a well-diversified and properly allocated portfolio with just two or three mutual funds—a total stock market fund, a total international stock market fund, and, since this example includes bonds, a total bond market fund.

Even simpler, you could use a target-date fund, which is a type of mutual fund offered by most fund companies. Just choose a fund with the year closest to your intended retirement date as part of its name. Planning to retire in or around 2060? Choose the Fidelity Freedom 2060 Fund (or the Vanguard Target Retirement 2060 Fund, or a similar fund from another fund company). The stock/bond mix will be what the fund company believes is appropriate for someone with that much time until retirement, and it'll automatically make the mix more conservative as you get older. Couldn't be simpler.

You could do something similar when investing for your children's college costs by using a 529 plan and choosing an age-based portfolio. Its asset allocation will be an appropriate stock/bond mix for someone your child's age, assuming a college start date at age eighteen. And, just like a target-date fund, it will automatically become more conservative as your child gets older.

2. DO IT YOURSELF WITH HELP

This option calls for subscribing to an investment newsletter, which will give you access to the publisher's proprietary strategies and investment recommendations. You'll maintain an account at the broker of your choice and make your own trades, but you'll do so guided by the recommendations in the newsletter. Just make sure the strategies are driven by clear, rules-based, objective processes, as opposed to thinly explained or subjective processes. Then choose a strategy that's appropriate for your time frame and risk tolerance. (Full disclosure: In my day job, I work for the publisher of an investment newsletter.)

3. USE A ROBO-ADVISOR

Many brokers offer what are referred to as *robo-advisory services*. After completing an online questionnaire that'll gather information about you, your goals, and your risk tolerance, you'll be presented with a recommended investment plan that the company will execute for you. The fee for using a robo-advisor is typically half or less what is charged by a human advisor.

4. CONSULT A HUMAN ADVISOR

This is the most customized way to invest, and usually the most expensive. In exchange for an annual fee based on a percentage of the amount of money you have the advisor manage for you, typically one percent or more, the advisor will meet with you, develop an investment plan tailored to your circumstances and goals, and manage all the buying and selling.

Stay with It

Of all the many risks we face as investors, the greatest one is letting our emotions get the best of us. Some of the hardest work of investing is being patient, battling fear, and hanging on during market storms.

At volatile times, remind yourself that you were intentional in choosing your investment strategy. It was designed with your age, goals, and investing temperament in mind, and it's adequately diversified. So trust it and stay with it.

Knowing some market history should help. While the US stock market has generated long-term average annual gains of about 10 percent, it hasn't moved up in a straight line. You should expect downturns, but the longer you stay invested, the more the odds of success move in your favor.[2]

Raising the Next Generation of Investors

Don't be afraid to introduce your kids to investing too early. Jon began talking about investing with his daughter, Claire, when she was just six. He taught her the basics of investing in stocks, that she could own small parts of companies she was familiar with. He even explained a little about how mutual funds work. He also taught her to understand some of how the market works, how it will go up and down but that you don't really lose money unless you sell when your investment has gone down in value. The longer you stay invested, the better your chances are of making money.

How much did she grasp? Apparently, quite a lot. She readily agreed to use some money she had saved to invest in a particularly aggressive mutual fund. One morning, as Jon prepared for work, he told his daughter that the market had been falling recently. She wasn't worried. In fact, she wrote him this note: "I said to keep my money in the fund." Jon kept the note and showed it to me. To see those words written in a six-year-old's handwriting made me smile. It was further proof that kids can understand more about money, including investing, at an earlier age than we sometimes assume.

Cast a Vision

To give your kids a sense of what's possible through investing, help them understand the power of compounding returns. As I mentioned in chapter 1, if you put one hundred dollars under your mattress every month, it will grow in a linear fashion (and you'll get a lumpy bed). Each step will be equal to the last. Your one-hundred-dollar stash will grow to two hundred dollars and then three hundred dollars. After fifty years, you'll have sixty thousand dollars.

But if you *invest* that money and generate an average annual return of 10 percent, it will grow exponentially. After fifty years, the sixty thousand dollars you've invested will have grown to more than $1.7 million. That example will give your kids a little taste of compounding, a force so powerful that Albert Einstein reportedly called it the eighth wonder of the world.

Compounding is the idea of a return on investment generating a return, and that return generating a return, and on and on. For example, if you invest one thousand dollars and earn a 10-percent return, after a year, you'll have $1,100. Your thousand dollars will have earned one hundred dollars. The next year, assuming you once again get a 10-percent return, you won't earn another hundred dollars—you'll earn $110. That's because your original thousand dollars earned 10 percent, and so did the hundred dollars you earned in the first year. Over time, a sum of money that earns a return—which then earns a return, which then earns a return—can turn into a lot of money.

Wealth gained hastily will dwindle,
but whoever gathers little by little will increase it.

PROVERBS 13:11

The three factors that fuel compounding are money, a rate of return, and time. Our kids may not have a ton of money available to them, but they *do* have time—and that's a very valuable advantage.

To demonstrate just *how* valuable it is, consider this. If our kids invested three thousand dollars at age eighteen and earned an average annual return of 12 percent, at age seventy their three thousand dollars will have turned into nearly $1.5 million. But what if they waited and invested three thousand dollars at age twenty-five instead of eighteen? Assuming that same average annual return of 12 percent, at age seventy they'd end up with about $650,000. By waiting just seven years, they'd miss out on $850,000. That's a big penalty for waiting even a little while.

By now you're probably wondering how they could earn 12 percent. There are certainly no guarantees, but the stock market is one viable option. Here's how.

Get Them Interested

With our kids, I like using financial mantras—money-related phrases I say often enough that I hope their messages stick. With investing, a mantra I like is "Why just buy what all the other kids buy when you could buy the companies that *make* what all the other kids buy?"

Let your kids know that they can become partial owners of companies they're familiar with by buying stock in those companies. Their ownership stake will be very, very small, of course, but they will become partial owners nonetheless.

Ask your kids what brands they like and why. Which ones do they see lots of other kids wearing? Which ones do they hear them talking about? Nike? Disney? Apple? Great! How about becoming partial owners of those companies?

While you could help your kids buy the individual stocks of such companies, it would take owning quite a few in order to be properly diversified, the idea we talked about earlier in which money is spread out across several investment options. So help them understand the value of mutual funds. While a mutual fund may seem more difficult to explain than a share of stock, remember, kids can understand more than we often assume. A *mutual fund* is an investment that holds many other investments, such as stocks or bonds. When you buy a share of a stock-based mutual fund, you become a partial owner of all the companies the mutual fund is invested in.

Today, it's never been easier or less expensive to buy shares of a type of mutual fund called an *exchange-traded fund* (ETF). Not long ago, you could only buy ETFs in whole-share amounts. If one share was valued at $150, that's the smallest amount you could invest. Plus, there was usually a commission. Today, several brokers offer fractional shares and don't charge commissions. That means your kids could invest in an ETF for as little as one dollar. That's amazing.

Open an Account

Legally, children can't have investment accounts in their own names until they reach the "age of majority," which is eighteen in most states and nineteen or twenty-one in others. But you can open a custodial account for them and make investments on their behalf. The assets will be transferred into their name once they reach the age of majority.

Fidelity is a good broker to use for such accounts because it doesn't charge a fee for opening an account, has no minimum opening balance requirement, sells fractional shares of ETFs, and offers custodial Roth IRAs (more on this soon).

Invest

Remember that time is a very valuable asset. The more time an investment has to compound, the better. Time also allows investors to take more risk in pursuit of greater gains. Our kids should have a lot of time, which is why I'm comfortable suggesting either of the following two investment ideas for them. Both are super simple in that each one uses a single stock-based ETF. Since they're ETFs, they are diversified across many individual holdings. Because they're *stock*-based ETFs, they are both aggressive, high-risk, high-potential-return funds.

The first option is an *S&P 500 index fund.* The S&P (Standard and Poor's) 500 is an index that replicates the collective stock performance of about five hundred large US-based companies. Among those companies are plenty your kids will recognize, such as Apple, Microsoft, Amazon, Meta (Facebook), Alphabet (Google), Tesla, Disney, and Nike. Because Fidelity offers S&P 500 ETFs in fractional shares, with as little as one dollar your kids could own very small stakes in each of those companies. The long-term average annual return of the S&P 500 has been about 10 percent. If that continues, three thousand dollars invested at age eighteen would be worth more than five hundred thousand dollars at age seventy.

If your kids got started at age sixteen, by age seventy their three thousand dollars would be worth nearly $650,000.

The second option is a *small-cap value index fund.* A small-cap value index fund invests in the stocks of smaller companies that by certain objective measures appear to be undervalued. While small-cap value funds are a bit riskier than S&P 500 funds, they have also generated better returns. Their long-term average annual return has been nearly 14 percent.[2] But let's be a little more conservative in our assumption. If an eighteen-year-old invested three thousand dollars in a small-cap value fund and it generated an average annual return of 12 percent, at age seventy it would be worth nearly $1.5 million. If your kids started at sixteen, by age seventy their portfolio would be worth nearly $1.9 million.[3]

Open a Second Account

As soon as your kids have *earned* income, open a second investment account for them—a custodial Roth IRA. Birthday money can't go into this account. What *can* go here is money they earn from jobs like mowing lawns, babysitting, dog walking, shoveling snow, or working in restaurants.

While Roth IRAs are intended for retirement, they come with some flexibility to access money earlier. Contributions may be withdrawn at any time and for any reason with no penalties or taxes due. Earnings may be accessed as well once an account has been open for at least five years and as long as the money is used for college or a first-time home purchase.

However, our kids will experience the real benefit of a Roth if they *don't* take money out early. If they keep it in there until retirement, they could end up with quite a bit of money and, as long as Congress doesn't change the law, all of it will be tax-free.

Also, having a Roth IRA won't count against them when it comes to determining eligibility for college financial aid.[4]

I know that retirement isn't the most exciting goal to pursue as a kid. It's so distant, so vague. And yet many people find themselves in later life with very little to live on. At their young age, our kids have an incredible opportunity to do things differently. They will never have a better opportunity to take such full advantage of the power of compounding.

I've told our kids that they don't have to do this but that I'd love to see them get two or three thousand dollars into a Roth IRA by the time they are sixteen to eighteen years old. The short-term pain of not being able to use this money for other things could create an amazing long-term gain. Once they have that Roth funded, they can largely forget about it and begin saving or investing for other things. So far, so good.

Necessary Cautions

The returns I mentioned are not guaranteed. All investing involves risk. And all investing, especially aggressive investing, will require our kids to have the emotional fortitude to stay invested even though their portfolios will surely have some bad years.

As they get older, our kids may want to reduce the risk in their retirement portfolios, which would reduce the assumed rate of return. Even so, they will be well on their way toward well-funded retirements.

Once our kids are working full-time, if their employers offer to match some of what they contribute to their workplace retirement plans, I would strongly encourage them to invest at least enough to capture that match. And they may want to invest more beyond that. But with the huge head start each one will have gotten on funding their retirement, they will have greater financial flexibility to give more, save for a house, start their own business, or pursue whatever other priority God puts on their heart.

Keep Teaching

One night, when Jonathan was fourteen, he asked for an update on his investments. So we went to the website of the broker where he and his two siblings have accounts. After checking his balance, he looked around some more, noticed lots of unfamiliar terms (like *cost basis*) and asked some great questions. If I had just tried to teach him about such terms, explaining that cost basis is how much a person initially pays for an investment, he probably wouldn't have been all that interested. But because he had some of his own real money invested, he wanted to learn. And that's the beauty of helping our kids get started with investing. It creates lots of real-world teaching moments.

Help Them Understand What They're Invested In and Why

I don't expect middle-schoolers to be able to explain the difference between a small-cap value fund and a large-cap growth fund. (Then again, some probably could.) But I think they should be able to explain that a mutual fund is an investment that holds lots of other investments. In other words, it's diversified, which is good because you never know which investments will do best and because diversification is a principle found in Scripture!

Let Them Experience Reality

It's one thing for our kids to see a chart of the market moving up and down. It's quite another for them to see the value of their own accounts moving up and down. As challenging as it can be for most investors to experience a significant downturn, it is a good teaching opportunity for our kids to go through such an experience while they're still under our roofs. We can teach them, as Jon taught his daughter, Claire, that you don't actually lose money unless you sell an investment when it's gone down in value. And we can remind them about the importance of maintaining a long-term view.

Now is the best time for our kids to start investing. For many of us adults, investing is the most confusing and intimidating of all financial subjects. But just as it's easier to learn how to ski when you're young, the same is true with investing. Let's have our kids grow up thinking it's normal to invest a portion of any money they receive, and let's make sure they get some hands-on experience. Helping our kids become investors is one more way we can get them thinking and acting like wise builders rather than consumers.

Sure, they could buy what all the other kids buy, but why not also buy the companies that make what all the other kids buy?

Recap and Next Steps

When investing, motives matter. It can be wise to invest in order to provide for our families in later life or to help our kids pay for college, but the Bible says it is foolish to invest in order to pursue a life of leisure. In order to invest well, develop a plan that includes a goal, its cost, the intended accomplishment date, and how much you'll need to invest each month to get there. You'll also need to know your investing temperament, or risk tolerance. Then select your account type (for retirement, will you use an IRA, a 401(k), or both?) and investment approach (DIY, DIY with help, robo-advisor, or human advisor). Use mutual funds, since they are inherently diversified. The biggest threat to your success is letting your emotions get the best of you. Choosing an investment approach that's appropriate for your time frame and temperament, along with knowing some market history, should help you weather the market's ups and downs.

- Don't be afraid to introduce the topic of investing to your kids too soon.

- Show your kids the incredible power of compounding and the advantage their young age gives them.

- Ask your kids, "Why just buy what all the other kids buy when you could buy the companies that make what all the other kids buy?" Let them know that they could become partial owners of companies they're familiar with.

- Help your kids understand the importance of diversification and introduce them to mutual funds, which are inherently diversified.

- Open a custodial account for your kids and help them start investing. Once they have earned income, open a custodial Roth account for them.

- Encourage your kids to memorize Proverbs 21:5: "Steady plodding brings prosperity; hasty speculation brings poverty" (TLB).

CHAPTER 8

SPENDING SMART

"One who is faithful in a very little is also faithful in much."
LUKE 16:10

I DON'T PARTICULARLY LIKE TO SHOP. So, for most of my life, if you had asked me about the most emotional experiences I've ever had, it would not have occurred to me to recall any of the times that I've gone shopping. To me, shopping is about knowing what I'm after and then getting in and out of the store as quickly as possible.

So it surprised me to find myself in an Old Navy store with tears in my eyes as I watched Annika and Andrew browse through racks of clothing, choose some things they wanted (and could afford), and then approach the cashier with what they had picked out in one hand and an envelope of cash in the other. I'll do my best to explain my odd reaction in a few minutes. First, let's look at many of our own spending decisions.

Less Is Not Always More

Don't worry—you're not in for a lecture on frugality. In fact, I don't even like that word. With apologies to those who do frugal well, to me, it conjures up images of miserly people obsessing about spending as little as possible, never leaving more than a 10 or 15 percent tip, and never splurging.

The phrase that motivates me more is *spending smart*. Within all spending categories are opportunities to do just that. Spending smart is about more than just getting the most for our money. It's also a spiritual issue. Everything belongs to God, so even the small financial decisions—shopping for groceries or deciding what to do this weekend—matter. And because spending money is the financial activity we do most often, our day-to-day uses of money give us frequent opportunities to teach our kids about managing it well.

Plus, let's face it: As kids get older, life gets more expensive. If we are to raise our kids in homes where there is a minimum of financial stress, we need to be in the game with our spending! Here are the main categories of spending in which we have opportunities to model wise spending to our kids.

Housing

This is most people's largest expense, so it's really important to get this one right. Spend well here and a house truly will be a home. Spend too much and your house will own you!

I'm just geeky enough to have run lots and lots of numbers, looking at how much money different-sized families across different income levels can afford to spend on a home. Here's my conclusion: For most, it's best to spend no more than 25 percent of monthly gross income on the combination of a mortgage, property taxes, and homeowner's insurance. Even better if we can keep that to no more than 20 percent. And here's the kicker: If you're a two-income household, it's best for that 20 to 25 percent to be from just one of those incomes. (At mattaboutmoney.com, you'll find recommended housing guidelines for various income levels.)

Is that an impossible goal? No. But it is challenging, especially since it runs hard against the grain of our consumer culture, the advice of Realtors and mortgage brokers, and what many of our friends have done. But it's definitely doable, and so incredibly helpful.

That 20-to-25-percent guideline plays a big role in enabling us to live generously, save and invest adequately, and enjoy one of life's most wonderful financial experiences: *margin*. Breathing space. A beautiful gap between our income and expenses.

As for basing that figure on one income: I once sat across the table from a couple who had built an expensive lifestyle that required both their incomes—a large mortgage, two financed vehicles, lots of dinners out. Then one of them lost their job. I saw fear and stress on their faces, plus what seemed like anger coming from the one who was still employed.

When Jude and I went through premarital counseling, the single best bit of financial advice we received was to build our lifestyle on just one of our incomes, and that's what we did. After renting for the first ten months of our marriage, we bought a condo in what our Realtor optimistically described as an "up and coming" neighborhood. It was pretty rough around the edges, but it was affordable on my income alone. We based our giving on our combined income, saved a significant portion of Jude's, and went on some great trips in those early years. Four years later, when Jonathan was born, it was relatively easy for us to live on one income, freeing Jude to leave her workplace job.

Even if you both plan to continue working, it's wise to buy a house you can afford on one income because it will give you a lot of options and keep stress levels low.

Property taxes are another factor to consider, especially if you haven't bought yet and have some flexibility in where you'll live. When we lived in Chicago, our last home was about 1,800 square feet and we paid over a thousand dollars a month in property taxes. That was a ton of money to spend on taxes. Today, our home in the Louisville area is larger, yet it cost less to buy and has property taxes that are less than half of what we used to pay.

As for homeowner's insurance: If it's been a while since you've shopped around, get a new quote or two. Also consider increasing your deductible. Just make sure you have enough in your emergency fund to cover it.

Maintenance and Repairs

The important point here is to include a monthly amount for these costs in your cash-flow plan. I recommend at least two hundred dollars per month, but it depends on the age and condition of your house. This money is for everything from furnace filters to light bulbs, and from mulch to leaky-pipe repairs. With a house, there's always something that needs fixing or maintaining. Some months you'll spend less than the amount you budgeted, but some months you'll spend a lot more. As I've reviewed people's budgets over the years, one of the most common mistakes is either not allocating any money for home (and vehicle) maintenance and repairs or not allocating enough.

Utilities

Have you compared cell-phone plan prices recently? If not, start with your current provider. Find out if you're on the most cost-effective plan. Also consider keeping your cell phones longer. New models seem to come out every month. Upgrading usually means increasing your monthly bill. And if you're among the few remaining households that still have a landline, consider dropping it and going cell-only.

There are other steps you can take to save on utilities as well. If you still have any old-fashioned incandescent light bulbs, wait until they burn out and then replace them with LED bulbs, which last longer and use less energy. Every little bit helps.

Transportation

You may notice that the transportation section of the cash-flow plan form on my website doesn't have a line item for a car payment. This goes in the debt section because I don't want you to *have* a car payment. If we're going to live lives of generosity and freedom, a car payment simply doesn't fit.

If you have a vehicle loan, make this the last car you ever finance. That means keeping it a long time, preferably fifteen years. Once it's paid off, redirect some or all of your monthly car payment to your big-ticket item replacement savings account.

When you need to buy a car, Consumer Reports is a good starting point for your research. It's a reputable source of information about which cars are most reliable. Then, on edmunds.com, you can find a True Cost to Own (TCO) tool, which shows the ongoing costs of different vehicles. Maybe you're trying to decide between two cars with similar purchase prices. The TCO tool can show you if one is less expensive to insure, maintain, and repair.

With vehicle insurance, just like homeowner's insurance, shop around to see if you have the best deal and consider raising the deductible. For vehicle maintenance and repairs, budget at least seventy-five dollars per month per vehicle.

SHOULD TEEN DRIVERS HAVE THEIR OWN CARS?

When your kids get to be driving age, I recommend encouraging them *not* to buy a car. Cars eat. They eat gasoline, insurance, maintenance, repairs, and sometimes parking tickets. If a young person is going to build savings, it helps a lot not to have a car. I realize that it may be more convenient for them (and you) if they were to have their own car, but try to make life work without another mouth to feed.

Food

Because we all buy food so often, grocery shopping with our kids presents lots of teaching moments (and opportunities for us to grow in patience!). Show them how to look for the cost-per-ounce or cost-per-count information on store shelves. Sometimes the larger size is more cost-effective; sometimes it isn't. Show them the cost difference between branded cereal and the store-brand version.

Introduce them to the soup section and point out that the types of soup are not in alphabetical order. That's intentional. Soup companies know that by forcing us to hunt through all the different types, we're more likely to buy additional cans.

Point out that the milk is often kept in the back of the store. Grocery store owners want us to shop all the way *to* this commonly purchased item so that we'll see lots of other tempting things to buy on the way back there. Also, show your kids that the most expensive brands are usually at eye level, so we should make sure to look up and down.

All these marketing techniques point to the importance of

using a shopping list and sticking to it. Also show your kids the coupons you're using and how much you can save with your frequent shopper card.

Clothing

Here, too, there are great opportunities to teach as we shop. My mom taught me to shop at quality stores but to buy only what's on sale. Today, I would never pay full price for an item of clothing. If I go to a department store, like Macy's, I only look at the sale racks. I also shop at T.J. Maxx or Marshalls, looking for good brands that are deeply discounted. One of my favorite stores is Nordstrom Rack, but even there I'll look for extra discounts.

Our son Andrew is very fashion-conscious. I've told him that there's nothing wrong with buying the brands he wants but that he'd be wise to look for what's on sale. He has gotten some great deals shopping the sale rack in the back room at Banana Republic. Recently, Jude introduced him and Annika to the wonders of thrift stores. She took them to a Goodwill store, where Andrew found three T-shirts he liked for two dollars each and Annika found a great sweater for five dollars. Go ahead, get the good stuff—just get it at a lower price.

Be intentional about staying off email marketing lists, and talk with your kids about marketing tactics in general. Point out how often a cashier will ask for your email address. They don't need it to process the transaction. They want to add you to the store's marketing list. Handing over your email address amounts to signing up for constant temptations to spend. And all the promotions have an urgency to them—maybe "supplies are limited" or "sale ends Thursday." Just say no to these tricks.

Of course, as with all spending, make sure you know how

He had discovered a great law of human action, without knowing it—namely, that in order to make a man or a boy covet a thing, it is only necessary to make the thing difficult to attain.

MARK TWAIN, *THE ADVENTURES OF TOM SAWYER*

much is still available in this month's clothing budget before you head to the store. One of my favorite financial mantras is "A deal isn't a deal unless it's a discount on something you were going to buy anyway." Getting a decent price on something that wasn't in your spending plan isn't really a deal. It's a budget buster.

Entertainment

Fun activities don't have to cost a lot of money. Go on bike rides or hikes; visit parks. Stream a movie rather than going to the theater, or go to a matinee instead of an evening showing. As much as you may enjoy going out to eat, consider a potluck dinner instead, which can be both fun and less expensive. Jude and I used to get together with several other couples for nationality-themed potluck dinners. We would rotate houses, with the host couple choosing the type of food and providing the entree. The other couples would bring side dishes, appetizers, and dessert. We got to try lots of new foods as we enjoyed each other's company.

Sports

While I haven't played much lately, golf is my favorite sport. In my bag are quality clubs from top brands, all of which I bought on deep discount. When new clubs are introduced, they cost a fortune. But if you're willing to buy the must-have gear from two or three years ago, it costs a lot less. Recently, I replaced a driver I've had for over fifteen years with a demo driver that was about two years old. The technology upgrade is amazing, and because the club was used, I got it for a great price.

If your kids are into sports, take them to used-sports-equipment stores or see what's available on Craigslist, eBay, or perhaps a community Facebook page.

Health Insurance

This has become one of the toughest categories on many family's cash-flow plans, including ours. Our family pays a fortune because we're on our own for health insurance. We're thinking about switching to a healthcare-sharing ministry.[1] I've heard nothing but good things from friends who have gone that route, so you might want to consider it as an option as well.

If your employer subsidizes your health insurance, be sure to make full use of a flexible savings account if you have access to one. Or consider using a high-deductible plan paired with a health savings account, which is what we're doing right now.

Life Insurance

With apologies to my friends in the life-insurance business, I can't think of many reasons why someone would need a whole-life policy. Term is much less expensive. You just have to realize that *term* means that you won't have it forever. When Jude was pregnant with Jonathan, we took out twenty-year level-premium term life-insurance policies on both of us. Several years ago, I picked up some more, wanting to make sure we have coverage at least until each of our kids is done with college.

Raising the Next Generation of Wise Spenders

How do we teach our kids to spend smart? It starts with taking them with us when we shop in stores or sitting them down with us when we shop online and talking them through what we're doing to spend wisely.

As they get older, the absolute best way I know of is to use an idea I learned from Mary Hunt in her book *Raising Financially Confident Kids*, where she tells the story of Uncle Harvey.[2] Harvey lived far away, so she hardly ever saw him. However, she had heard some unusual stories about him, and when she and her husband, Harold, were raising their two boys, the legend of Uncle Harvey loomed large.

They knew that at the start of each year, Harvey would sit down with his family and hand out a year's worth of money to each of his four sons. The money was for clothing, snacks, entertainment, haircuts—pretty much everything but housing and groceries. It was up to them to make it last. If they ran out of money before they ran out of year, too bad. And, the Hunts heard, each of Harvey's kids grew up to be very good money managers.

It prompted Mary and Harold to give it a try with their boys. In her book, she explains how they rolled out the plan with their sons, some of the early fits and starts, and how it all turned out. I liked the idea so much that we decided to try it with our kids when they were nine, eleven, and fourteen. That's what led to the story I started to tell at the beginning of this chapter.

We had budgeted twenty-five dollars per month per child for clothing, so we decided to give them that money in cash each month. They each kept the money in an envelope and recorded the monthly inflow and each expenditure on the outside.

On our trip to Old Navy, Annika was in search of some jeans.

Andrew had said that he didn't really need anything. (But he likes clothing, so I wondered whether he could really go to a clothing store and not buy anything.) After trying on several pairs of jeans, Annika decided on one pair that was being offered on a nice discount. Then we headed over to the deep-discount rack, where she found two tops for about two dollars each.

At that point, Andrew said that he wanted to buy something after all. I reminded him that he had said he didn't need anything. But he insisted that he could use a new sweatshirt. He picked one out that was 30 percent off but still seemed kind of expensive to me and looked a lot like one he already owned.

Still, I backed off, wanting him to make his own decisions. I figured that if he later regretted the purchase . . . well, that's part of what this is all about.

I can't fully put into words the fascination and joy I experienced as I watched each one navigate this process. They were clearly thinking and making decisions about purchases in a way that was new to them.

Of course, they had bought things before, but there was something different about this. I guess it's that they were taking responsibility for a new financial category. They had certainly been with us as we'd shopped for clothes for them and had helped pick out what they wanted. But this time they were much more in charge, and it was all much more real. They had a finite amount of money in hand, which made the spending limit more tangible. Being the ones to hand over cash themselves is very different from having us buy the clothing with a credit card and manage a "kids clothing" budget on their behalf.

I think what made it so moving for me was seeing the funnel we talked about in the introduction in action. Our kids were growing up. As planned, the funnel was opening up. And they were stepping up to this new level of responsibility. Watching it all play out was wonderful, and more than a little bittersweet. We really *were* putting ourselves out of a job.

Taking It up a Notch

Parents Karen and David did something very similar with their daughter, Rachel. They started giving her an allowance when she was about five. Then, when she was in the seventh grade, they decided to take things to a whole new level.

"We thought, *We have six years before she will be off to college,*" Karen said. "*Let's see what we can teach her in that time about what it's like to live as an adult with real responsibilities.*"

That year, they increased Rachel's allowance and gave her responsibility for buying her own clothing. Then, each year on her birthday, they increased her allowance some more and gave her responsibility for a new spending category. One year it was personal-care items, like toiletries and makeup. Then it was entertainment, including even her portion when they went out to eat as a family.

Rachel, now in her midtwenties, said, "That entertainment one really got me. It made me realize how expensive it is to go out." Some weeks, she had to choose between having dinner at a restaurant with her parents, whom she's always been very close to, or going to the movies with her friends. She didn't have enough money to do both—and that was the point.

"This was all about helping her learn to be an adult," Karen said, "so that when she went off to college, she would make good choices." In part, the financial training plan was born out of Karen's experience growing up. When she'd learned how to drive, her dad had taught her how to change a tire and even change the oil, which she points out are skills she's never had to use. But she wasn't taught how to manage money, which is a skill we all have to use every day. She remembers going off to college and in November running out of the spending money she'd thought would last her through the next spring.

Rachel said, "I'm very grateful my parents taught me how to budget and make some of those hard choices, because I never had one of those crisis moments in college when I had to say, 'I'm out of money. What am I going to do now?'"

Toward the end of Rachel's senior year of high school, her parents added one final step to her money-management training. They had her take over the family budget, paying all household bills and balancing the checkbook.

"We wanted her to see what the other expenses were," Karen explained. "It's easy for kids to feel like their parents have unlimited money. But when you see where it all goes, it can be very eye-opening."

There are various ways to implement a plan like this. Uncle Harvey handed out all the cash for the year at once. Mary and Harold and Karen and David parsed it out monthly, which is what Jude and I are doing. Mary and Harold started the plan when each of their boys was in the sixth grade. Karen and David started when their daughter was in the seventh. We started all three of our kids at the same time when our oldest was in the eighth grade and our youngest was in the third. The categories you choose to give your kids responsibility for may vary, but clothing seems like a natural starting point.

Don't worry about devising the perfect plan. The important thing is to give your kids more and more responsibility for spending decisions and embrace your gatekeeper role by avoiding the temptation to intervene if they make bad decisions. The pain of regret is one of the best teachers.

Key Lessons

If you decide to do something similar with your kids, and I hope you will, look for opportunities to teach the following skills.

KNOW WHAT YOU'RE RESPONSIBLE FOR

When they took their kids to the pool, parents Amy and Ling would bring crackers or popcorn from home. At first, their kids were envious of the other kids, whose parents would give them money for snacks. "So sometimes they would bring their own money to spend," said Amy. "But they soon realized how expensive it was and how they *didn't* want to spend all their money on candy or a soda just because someone else was doing it. I never told them they couldn't—just that I wouldn't finance it."

MANAGE TO THE NUMBER

Your kids should know how much they can spend on clothing or personal-care items or whatever else *before* they get to the store. Having a spending limit is healthy. It will help them learn many of the following skills on this list.

ACCOUNT FOR TAXES

Having to pay sales tax can be another tough introduction to the real world. One father, Neil, taught his young boys to prepare for it and gave them grace a couple of times when they forgot, but at a certain point he drew the line. "They would go to buy a pack of gum and wouldn't have enough. The hardest thing for me was not putting down a dime to cover it, but they had to learn. And from then on, they knew I wasn't going to bail them out. If they didn't have enough, they didn't even ask. They just put it back."

MAKE TRADE-OFFS

Another example of facing reality is when you realize you can't buy everything you want, so you have to make a choice. Two inexpensive toys or one more expensive toy? These two inexpensive shirts now or this more expensive one now and that more expensive one next month?

COMPARISON SHOP

When Rachel was about seven years old, if she wanted to buy something, her parents required her to get three prices and wait a week. Very often, Karen said, "by the time she had gotten three prices, she didn't want it anymore. She learned early on that many of the things that were shiny in her mind wouldn't stay shiny. And she learned that without having to buy them first."

COST VS. VALUE

Help your kids notice what brands hold up best and which ones tend to wear out or break quickly. The lesson? The lowest-priced option is not necessarily what'll be least expensive in the long run.

WHEN POSSIBLE, NEGOTIATE

When Andrew was eight, he had been saving for a Star Wars LEGO set. One day, we found out that a used-LEGO store had opened up in our town and decided to go. Surprisingly, it had a used version of the exact set he had been saving for, and it was priced much lower than a new one. I whispered in his ear that he should offer even less. So he did, and the store manager agreed. A lot of people are hesitant to ask for deals. Giving our kids some early experience with this can give them confidence.

SPEAK UP

Jonathan was also into LEGO. When he was six, the company was selling individually packaged figures ("minifigs") for what seemed like a good price. The only catch was that the packaging prevented you from seeing which one you were buying. From the company's perspective, maybe it was a good marketing technique, but when Jonathan bought three and ended up with two that were the same, he felt ripped off. So I helped him find a customer-service phone number. When he called, he earnestly expressed his disappointment at ending up with two of the same minifig and went on to suggest that they make the packaging transparent. The customer-service rep listened very politely and then sent him a free minifig.

PAPER OR PLASTIC?

The other day, Jude took our kids to buy some clothing. When the cashier saw that they planned to pay with cash, he had to call his manager over for help. Apparently, the use of cash is becoming so rare that it requires a special procedure in this store.

We are becoming an increasingly cashless society. For however long as it's still possible, I like the idea of having young kids use cash. It's simply more real, more tangible. But eventually, it'll be important to teach them to use today's more common payment methods, beginning with debit cards.

There's no hard-and-fast rule as to what age is best, but we plan to get Jonathan and Andrew set up with checking accounts and debit cards this year while Jonathan is a senior in high school (arguably, later than is ideal) and Andrew a sophomore (probably about right, although a year earlier would have been fine.) We want them to learn to stick to a budget while paying in a more abstract way than with cash, monitor the electronic inflows and outflows, and keep tabs on the whereabouts of their debit cards.

The combination of giving our kids responsibility for new spending categories (such as clothing) and getting them started with checking accounts presents a good opportunity to have them learn how to use online budgeting tools, like Mint. While there will be a learning curve in creating a budget and categorizing expenses properly, since kids grow up using technology, they will figure it out quickly.

In the next chapter, we'll turn our attention to the most common financial issue plaguing adults: debt. Drawing from my own experience, I'll offer some guidance on getting out of debt if that's your situation. Then we'll explore ways to help our kids grow up with healthy beliefs and behaviors around credit and debt.

Recap and Next Steps

Spending is the financial activity we all do most often, so it presents many opportunities to teach our kids about wise money management. But first things first: In order for us to be good role models, and in order for our kids to grow up in low-financial-stress environments, it's important that we spend well. We'll get the most bang for the buck by starting with the highest-cost areas, such as housing (trying to keep the combination of a mortgage, property taxes, and homeowner's insurance to a maximum of 25 percent of monthly gross income) and transportation (ideally, paying cash for cars). Within every spending category are opportunities to spend smart, which means being intentional about our spending.

- Show your kids how you shop at the grocery store (using a list, comparing cost per ounce or per count, using coupons and/or a frequent shopper card)

- Show your kids how you shop at the clothing store (buying quality items that are on sale, making trade-offs).

- Starting perhaps as early as the third grade, begin using the "Uncle Harvey" method of teaching kids about wise money management. Give them the money you would have spent on them for clothing along with the responsibility for managing that money. Over time, do the same for other spending categories, such as entertainment or toiletries.

- At first, have your kids use cash. Sometime in high school, get them set up with checking accounts and debit cards, which will teach them some new skills, such as monitoring electronic inflows and outflows and keeping tabs on their debit cards. This is a good time to get them started with an online budgeting tool as well.

- Encourage your kids to memorize Luke 16:10: "One who is faithful in a very little is also faithful in much."

CHAPTER 9

BORROWING CAUTIOUSLY

You were bought for a price;
do not become slaves of people.
I CORINTHIANS 7:23, NASB

Do you know why young kids often seem so carefree? Why they smile and laugh so easily? Why, when they have somewhere to go, they often run or skip? No debt. They don't have to worry about making mortgage payments, keeping up with credit-card bills, covering car payments, or paying off student loans (at least not yet!). Dealing with debt is just not part of a child's growing-up experience.

What if it wasn't part of their *grown-up* experience either? At the very least, what if it wasn't a *burdensome* part of it? It doesn't have to be. But the seeds of debt- and credit-related attitudes and behaviors are planted early in life, so it's an important topic for us to teach our kids through conversation, by example, and—you may be surprised to hear me suggest—through experience. We'll get to that in a few minutes.

One Great Gift

As I've mentioned, several financial habits I developed early in life contributed mightily to the trouble I got into with debt later on. While I built a strong work ethic, I developed an equally strong love of spending. When I discovered credit cards, which let me buy lots of stuff without having to pay for much of it right away, I was all about it. I had to learn the hard way that it's really easy to get into debt and really hard to get out.

Although God used the mistakes I made in positive, life-changing ways, I don't necessarily recommend the route I took. As we have in most chapters, before we talk about our kids, let's look at debt and credit through adult eyes.

If you have a credit-card balance you carry from month to month, education debt, a vehicle loan, or another type of debt (other than a reasonable mortgage), let me encourage you to get out from under that debt sooner rather than later. In our culture, having debt is the norm, a fact that goes a long way toward explaining why people generally give so little, don't have enough in their savings or investment accounts, and live with so much stress.

Within marriage, debt is a happiness killer. According to Utah State researcher Jeffrey Dew, consumer debt "fuels a sense of financial unease among couples," increasing the likelihood that they will fight over money, argue about other issues, and spend less time together.[1] It will be a great benefit to your marriage and a wonderful gift to your kids if you live free of debt. Here's how.

1. Find Out Where You Are

If you have debt, enter the details in the Accelerated Debt Payoff Calculator on my website (mattaboutmoney.com). This includes credit-card balances that you carry from month to month, student loans, auto loans, and any others. Feel free to include your mortgage if it's a priority for you to accelerate your payments on that. Enter the debts in order, from the one with the lowest balance to the one with the highest.

- *Vehicle debt.* If we're going to live generously and save and invest adequately, a vehicle payment won't fit on our cash-flow plans. So if you have a vehicle loan, I would encourage you to add it to your Accelerated Debt Payoff plan and commit to making this the last vehicle you ever finance.

- *Student-loan debt.* The standard repayment term for federal student loans is ten years, but there's no reason to put up with a loan for that long. Make its early payoff part of your Accelerated Debt Payoff plan as well, especially since there is no penalty for paying more than the required monthly amount on a student loan.

2. Go No Further into Debt

Decide right now that you will take on no more debt. If that means removing your credit cards from your wallet or purse to keep temptation at bay, do that. If it means cutting them up, do that.

3. Commit to Getting Out and Staying Out of Debt

Print and sign the Debt-Free Commitment Form you'll find on my website. This may seem unnecessary, insignificant, or even silly, but it isn't. There's something powerful about signing our names to a commitment, especially a commitment to a goal that may be difficult to achieve.

4. Go Public with Your Commitment

This will be the most uncomfortable part of the process, and the most helpful. Approach a trusted friend or family member, tell them about your debt and your commitment to pay it off, and ask them to be your encouragement and accountability partner. If you're married, you and your spouse will be each other's partner in this journey, but each of you should find one other person as well. Have these accountability partners also sign the Debt-Free Commitment Form. Invite them to ask you about your progress from time to time and to pray for you regularly.

5. Fix and Roll Your Payments

If you have an education or vehicle loan, it's an *installment loan*. You'll pay the same amount each month for a set number of months.

A credit-card balance that you carry from month to month is a *revolving loan*. There is no fixed payment amount or payoff date. If you take on no more debt and make the required minimum payment each month, then each month that required minimum payment amount will decrease a little bit.

Isn't that kind of the credit-card company? Of course, it isn't kindness. It's math. Your minimum payment is based on your balance. If your balance is going down a little each month, so will your required minimum payment. Making this declining minimum payment is what will keep you in debt for approximately . . . forever!

Let's say you have a three-thousand-dollar balance on a credit card that charges 18-percent interest and requires a minimum payment of 2 percent of the balance or fifteen dollars, whichever is higher. If you make the required minimum payment each month, it'll take you nearly thirty-one years to pay it off! And you'll end up paying almost $7,400 in interest. Talk about the borrower being "servant to the lender" (Proverbs 22:7, TLB)!

One simple step you can take toward getting out of debt faster is to fix your payments. With our three-thousand-dollar example where the required minimum monthly payment is 2 percent of the balance, that's sixty dollars. Next month, when the credit-card company asks for just $59.70, keep paying sixty dollars. If you pay sixty dollars each and every month, you'll be out of debt in under eight years, and you'll pay about $2,600 in interest. That's a big improvement for very little effort.

The "roll" part of this step is that once you completely pay off one debt, take the full amount you were paying on that debt and roll it into the payment for your next-lowest-balance debt.

LOWEST BALANCE OR HIGHEST INTEREST?

You may be wondering whether it's really best to prioritize your lowest-balance debt over your highest-interest-rate debt. While going after your highest-interest debts first will get you out of debt *a little* faster and cost you *a little* less interest, there's something very motivating about completely wiping out one of your debts as quickly as possible.[2] That's why I recommend going after your lowest-balance debts first.

6. Accelerate Your Payments

Fixing and rolling your payments will speed up the process of getting out of debt. Adding more to the fixed minimum will *really* speed things up. Using the Accelerated Debt Payoff Calculator, try different added amounts—ten or twenty or one hundred dollars per month—and find out how much more quickly you'll be out of debt. (Add those amounts where it says, "Enter a monthly dollar amount you can add to your debt-payoff plan.")

In our example, if you fix your payments at one hundred dollars instead of sixty dollars per month, you'll be out of debt in about three and a half years. Fix it at two hundred dollars, and you'll be out of debt in one and a half years. Either way, you'll also spend a lot less on interest.

Hopefully, seeing how much more quickly you could be out of debt by adding to your fixed minimums will motivate you to find the money. As I suggested earlier, if you use 10 to 15 percent of your monthly gross income to build an emergency fund totaling one month's worth of essential living expenses and then redirect that amount toward accelerating the payoff of your debts, that should really speed up the process of becoming debt free.

There are many other ways to free up money to put toward your debts as well. For example, you could go on an entertainment-spending fast for the next year by looking for fun, free things to do in your area. Consider canceling your streaming subscriptions, or at least stepping down to less expensive plans. For the next six to twelve months, commit to buying no new clothes except what's truly necessary. (I know someone who went on a spending fast across all her spending categories, buying only the essentials for a year. Not only did it help her accomplish her goal, but when she ended the fast, she found that it had permanently reordered her spending priorities.) Once you figure out your accelerated debt payoff amount, add it to your lowest-balance debt while keeping all your other payments fixed. Once that debt is paid off, roll the full amount into the next-lowest-balance debt and keep going.

Continue doing that, and one day you'll find yourself completely out of debt. That will be one amazing day!

7. Stay the Course

Having a budget and maintaining an emergency fund are important keys to staying out of debt, as is always remembering who you are—a wise builder, not a consumer. Your journey out of debt is about getting the facts of your financial situation in alignment with who you are.

The Wise Use of Credit Cards

If you've decided not to use credit cards, don't let me talk you into using them. On the other hand, if you *do* use credit cards, here are my rules of the road for using them responsibly.

1. Use Them Only for Preplanned, Budgeted Items

If you don't use a cash-flow plan, don't use credit cards. However, if you have a plan that enables you to live generously and save and invest adequately, credit cards can work just fine. Let's say you've budgeted seventy-five dollars per month for clothing. You can charge seventy-five dollars' worth of clothing each month.

2. Record Your Spending as You Spend

If you don't track your cash flow, do not use credit cards. However, if you do, and if you record each credit-card purchase *when you make that purchase*, credit cards can be a useful tool. Even though you don't actually spend money out of your checking account when you charge something on a credit card, it's important to treat each transaction as if you did. That seventy-five dollars you spent on clothing with a credit card counts against *this month's* clothing budget. That way, seventy-five dollars sitting in your checking account is spoken for and unavailable for any other use.

If you use an electronic cash-flow tracking tool (like Mint), your credit-card spending will be tracked automatically, and each transaction will count against this month's budgeted amount for the category. If you charge one hundred dollars when buying groceries, you just spent one hundred dollars of this month's groceries budget. If you use a manual tracking system (like an Excel spreadsheet or a paper-and-pencil system), you'll have to remember to record your spending each time you use your credit card.

No matter what budgeting tool you use, counting a credit-card purchase against this month's budgeted amount means that you should use your budget as the guide for how much you can continue to spend each month, not the balance in your checking account. The seventy-five dollars you spent on clothing won't actually come out of your checking account until you pay the credit-card bill next month.

This track-it-as-you-charge-it step is crucial. The people who get in trouble with credit cards are the ones who don't track what they charge and are then shocked when they get their bill and can't imagine having charged so much over the last thirty days.

3. Pay Your Balance in Full Each Month

Never carry a balance. If you have a balance on a credit card that you carry from month to month, don't use credit cards. Paying interest on credit-card charges is one of the absolute worst uses of money there is. It's very easy to dig yourself deep into debt by making purchases and then paying the minimums. And then, as I know, it's really, really tough to pay it off. Don't go there. However, if you take the first two steps *and* always pay your bill in full each month, credit cards can be part of a healthy relationship with money.

4. If You Won't Take the First Three Steps, Don't Use Credit Cards

Those who say that no one should use a credit card point to studies showing that people who use them tend to spend more than those who don't. I get that. Paying with a piece of plastic feels abstract. At a fast-food restaurant, it's much easier to say yes to the large fries and drink when you're charging your meal instead of paying with cash. We would all be wise to keep that reality in mind. *And*, as long as you take the steps outlined above, you should be able to use credit cards in a way that keeps your spending within your plan.

The Benefits of Credit Cards

Used responsibly, credit cards come with several benefits. First and foremost, they provide better security than debit cards. If someone steals your debit card and PIN, fraudulent purchases or withdrawals will come straight out of your checking account. While many issuers have zero-liability policies, it can take time to restore the money. Meanwhile, the lower balance in your account may leave you unable to pay bills.

With credit cards, fraudulent purchases *do not* come out of your checking account; they show up on your statement, giving you time to notify the issuer that the purchases were not yours.

There are other credit-card benefits as well, from extended warranties to rental-car insurance to points that can be turned into cash, airline tickets, and more. As I said, don't let me talk you into using them if you prefer not to, but there *is* such a thing as the wise use of credit cards.

Raising the Next Generation
of Wise Users of Credit and Debt

Our main gatekeeper role here is to not loan money to our kids. If their allowance money runs out and they ask for an advance on next week's allowance, just say no. If there's a great deal on something they desperately want but it would require them needing to borrow some money from you, just say no.

> *A limit is generally not loved the first time around—*
> *or for that matter, the first several times around.*
>
> DR. HENRY CLOUD AND DR. JOHN TOWNSEND, *BOUNDARIES WITH KIDS*

As with so many of the nos we have to deliver as parents, this one will be tough sometimes. Stick to your guns. Get your kids in the habit of thinking like planners and savers, not borrowers.

When your kids are about middle-school age, show them just how dangerous debt can be. Use the example I mentioned earlier that shows what happens when people get compounding working against them. In the same way positive compounding could turn an investment of three thousand dollars when your child is eighteen into more than a million dollars by the time they retire, negative compounding could turn three thousand dollars of credit-card debt into more than ten thousand dollars of debt, hanging around like a ball and chain strapped to their ankles for nearly thirty-one years.[3]

Think of compounding as a powerful financial fan. It's helpful when the wind is at your back, as it is with investing. It's a hindrance when it's in your face, as with debt.

A Credit-Card Learner's Permit

Now that you've established in your kids the habit of not borrowing and have given them a scary look at the dangers of debt, get them a credit card. Wait, what? That's right, before they leave home, I recommend getting them a credit card.

Just because people get into car accidents doesn't mean we shouldn't allow our kids to drive once they're old enough. It should motivate us to do all that we can to teach them how to drive safely. It's the same with credit cards. I'd rather have our kids learn the wise use of credit cards while they're under our roofs. If they will follow the four steps for the wise use of credit cards that I described earlier, they should be just fine.

SET YOUR CHILDREN UP AS AUTHORIZED USERS

By law, no one can get a credit card in their own name without a co-signer until they are twenty-one years old. However, chances are good that you could make your child an authorized user of one of your cards. Different issuers have different rules about this. Some allow children as young as twelve to become authorized users, others not until age eighteen. When your child is a junior or senior in high school is about the right time.

As an authorized user, your child will get a card in their name, but it'll be tied to your account. There are two main benefits to making your child an authorized user. First, it will enable them to establish a credit history and credit score. This will be helpful to them when they apply to rent an apartment in the future. Eventually, it will impact their ability to qualify for a mortgage and the rate at which they can do so. In addition, prospective employers sometimes check credit reports, although they need permission and cannot access credit scores.

Be sure to check with your issuer to make sure information about the card will be reported to the credit bureaus using your child's Social Security number. Only then will your child build a credit history. Also, only consider doing this if your credit score is strong, because your credit history will impact theirs.

TEACH YOUR KIDS THAT THEIR CREDIT SCORE IS THEIR FINANCIAL REPUTATION

Scores range from 300 to 850. The higher, the better. A score between 690 to 719 is considered good; 720 or higher is excellent. The most important of five factors that impact credit scores is your history of paying your bills on time. The second is your credit utilization, which is how much of your available credit you're using.[4] For this purpose, it doesn't matter whether you pay your entire balance each month (although you should do that). The credit bureaus simply take a look at some point in the month to see how much of your credit limit you are using at that moment. Utilizing less than 30 percent of available credit is good, less than 10 percent is even better.

CHECK YOUR CREDIT SCORE

You should be able to get your credit score for free from your bank, credit union, or credit-card issuer. Look on their website or give them a call to find out what it is.

CHECK YOUR CREDIT REPORTS

To get your reports, go to annualcreditreport.com. You are entitled to one free report from each of the three credit bureaus once a year. Review your reports with your kids so they can see what's included in them. Especially if your credit score is below the "good" level (690), look to see if there are any errors on the report. If so, the report will explain what to do.

SEE IF YOUR KIDS HAVE A CREDIT REPORT

Even if your kids have never used credit, check to see if any of them have a credit report. If they do, someone may have gotten hold of their Social Security number and used it to open a credit account. For children age thirteen or older, you can just enter their information, including their Social Security number, at annualcreditreport.com. If they are younger, you'll have to make the request by mail. The best scenario would be that they don't have a credit report. If they do, information for initiating an investigation will be on each credit report.

The second main benefit of adding your child as an authorized user is that it will give them some practice using a credit card. Review with your child the four rules of the road for the wise use of credit cards described earlier. Maybe you're giving them fifty dollars per month for clothing. They can charge fifty dollars' worth of clothing in a given month.[5]

Keep in mind that an authorized user is not legally responsible for the purchases they make. So consider using a contract between you and your child that spells out the terms.[6] Use it to make clear what they can use the card for, that they need to get your approval before they use the card (at least for the first several months), and that they are agreeing to meet with you every month when you receive the bill to go over the past month's charges and pay you for what they've charged.

Paying for College

Student loans are often a young person's first experience with debt, and all too often, it's a rude awakening. Start talking with your kids about college at least by the time they are in middle school. Do they think they'll want to go to college? Would you like them to go? What are the alternatives? Community college? A trade school? The military?

If they plan to go to college, help them understand how much it's likely to cost, and let them know how much of the cost they are going to be responsible for. Talk with them about factors that will impact the cost, such as whether they go to an in-state or out-of-state school and whether they go to a public or private school.

Show them the implications of student loans. For example, if college is likely to cost one hundred thousand dollars for four years (very realistic for an in-state public school), and if they borrow twenty thousand dollars, that will translate into a monthly cost of about two hundred dollars they'll have to pay for ten years.[7] That's a big monthly bill for a long time. Especially as they get closer to college age and have a better feel for what they want to study, show them estimates of starting salaries in that field,[8] help them rough out a first-year-post-college budget, and show them the implications of a student-loan payment.

Hopefully, all this will motivate our kids to save as much as possible toward their college costs and influence their decisions about where to apply.

The Lessons of Your Life

What's the best way to raise our kids with a healthy perspective about credit and debt? First, if you use credit cards, follow the four rules of the road for their wise use described earlier. Second, live as free of debt as possible—no credit-card balances carried from month to month, no vehicle loans, and no student loans. The only "acceptable" type of debt is a reasonable mortgage. Talk with your kids about debt-related decisions you've made and why. I have told our kids that I am more than content to drive an older, paid-off car because it frees us to spend money on things we value more, like family vacations.

If you have debt, it may take some time to pay it off. It took me four and a half years to pay off all my credit-card debt and another year to wipe out my vehicle loan. But it's possible, and your debt-free life will speak volumes, teaching your kids an uncommon, countercultural, and priceless lesson in wise money management.

Recap and Next Steps

One of the greatest gifts you could give your kids is to live as free from debt as possible. Living free from the bondage of debt is an unusual way to live—an unusually good way to live! It will require patience and resistance to the pull of the culture, but it will do wonders for your peace of mind while setting a powerful example for your kids.

- Do not lend money to your kids. Condition them to be planners and savers, not borrowers.

- Show your kids how long it will take and how much it will cost to pay off a credit-card balance over time.

- When your child is a junior or senior in high school, consider getting them set up as an authorized user on one of your credit cards, and then teach them how to use it wisely. It'll be better for them to learn while they're still under your roof than when they are out on their own.

- Teach your kids about credit scores (their financial reputation) and credit reports.

- As you begin talking with each of your kids about college, show them the implications of education loans so that this knowledge informs their choice of a college and motivates them to do everything possible to avoid having to borrow money.

- Encourage your kids to memorize 1 Corinthians 7:23: "You were bought for a price; do not become slaves of people" (NASB).

Section III

Stepping Back

Two Final Lessons for
a Healthy Lifelong
Relationship with Money

CHAPTER 10

OUR INNER MONEY MANAGER

I praise you, for I am fearfully and wonderfully made.
Wonderful are your works;
my soul knows it very well.

PSALM 139:14

WHEN ANDREW WAS ELEVEN, he would ask me somewhat regularly about my dream car—what I'd love to drive someday in the future. I told him several times that owning an especially nice car isn't a big deal to me. What I value in a car is reliability and low cost.

That answer never satisfied him, so he kept bringing it up. He'd ask whether I'd prefer a Lamborghini or a Ferrari (realistic options, right?). I'd explain that I'm perfectly happy with my eleven-year-old Honda Accord. I might as well have been speaking a foreign language. Some time would pass, and then he'd ask again: "Corvette or Camaro?" He simply couldn't understand how anyone could be so unenthusiastic about the possibility of owning a cool car.

He is a classic sanguine. That's his primary temperament. He has all the signs. He's outgoing, charming, and makes friends easily. If he had a motto, it would be "Everything goes better with other people." He likes team sports and group activities. I learned very quickly that when he asks me for help with his homework, he doesn't really need help; he just wants company. And he cares about his appearance. He knows what he likes—which clothing brands, how to style his hair, and, yes, what type of car he'd like to own one day—preferably a sports car or an off-road vehicle, but it has to be just the right color.

As I'm writing this chapter, Andrew is fifteen. One day, I realized I couldn't remember him asking me about cars recently and wondered if that had become less important to him than when he was eleven. The very day I started thinking about it, as if on cue, he asked me, "Dad, what's your dream car?"

While he isn't managing a lot of money right now, he'll manage more as he gets older. And he will discover, with some help from me, how his temperament influences how he sees and uses money.

Temperament may be the most underrated, underappreciated factor that influences how we manage money. In essence, our *temperament* is our nature, especially as it affects our behavior. The late Tim LaHaye, a former pastor and author who wrote extensively about temperament, described it as "the unseen force underlying human action."[1]

Temperament goes a long way toward explaining why some people have a hard time building savings and others tend to save too much. It's why some people are quick to give and others are stingy, why some are more comfortable taking risks with their investments and others prefer to play it safe. Temperament has a lot to do with why some people are especially prone to buying things impulsively, overspending in general or on particular things (like clothing), being hesitant to finalize purchasing decisions, hounding the people they love about how *they're* spending, and more.

Oftentimes, when you have a disagreement with your spouse, the issue isn't really what you're raising your voice about; it's a clash of temperaments. Understanding your God-given temperament and your spouse's is hugely helpful in managing money effectively and in doing so as a team. Helping our kids understand their temperaments and how this impacts their use of money will be very beneficial to them as well.

What's Your Type?

There are several different temperament-classification systems, but they all trace back to the one formulated by Hippocrates (the father of modern medicine) all the way back in 370 BC, which was then refined by the Roman physician Galen in AD 190. This system consists of four temperaments: sanguine, choleric, melancholy, and phlegmatic.

Everyone has a primary and a secondary temperament. In some people, their primary temperament is especially dominant. In others, their primary and secondary temperaments are more balanced, with one playing a larger role in certain situations and the other being more dominant under different circumstances.

You can't choose to switch to a different temperament. You were born with the one you have, and you'll have it all your days. However, you can learn to manage your temperament. That's good news, because each temperament comes with some inherent strengths and weaknesses. It also means that we can't go around blaming our temperaments for any bad behavior. Yes, they'll get the best of us sometimes, but we're not helpless victims. If we work at it, we can each gain some control over our temperament.

Of course, in order to take full advantage of your temperament's inherent strengths and not live at the effect of its inherent weaknesses, you have to know what it is. To identify yours, go through the next few pages and take note of the characteristics that best describe you. You can also find a temperament test at mattaboutmoney.com/resources. Put a check mark next to the characteristics that describe you, and then count up how many check marks you have in each of the four groupings. The column with the most check marks is your primary temperament; the one with the second most is your secondary temperament.

For each of your children, starting in their early to mid-teens, understanding their temperament and some of the tendencies that come with it will be a big help to them in learning how to manage money well and much more. We'll get to that in a minute. First, here's an adult-eyed look at each of the four temperaments, some of the tendencies associated with them, how those tendencies may play out in managing money, and some ideas for managing your temperament.

Sanguine

If you've ever been described as a people person, your primary temperament may be *sanguine*. Outgoing, warm, friendly, full of faith, and expressive of their emotions, sanguines are fun to be around. They're great conversationalists and engaging storytellers.

Sanguines tend to be free spenders, making financial decisions by feel, not by plan. When spending on themselves, their tastes tend toward the flashy, what's in style, and popular brands. They are also quick to spend on others and are the most generous of the four temperaments.

If you're married to a sanguine, I wouldn't hold out hope that they will one day develop a passion for analytics. As Tim LaHaye quipped, "I have never met a sanguine accountant."[2] That doesn't give them a pass on the budgeting process, though. You should both be involved in deciding how much of your income you're going to give, save, and invest; how much you're going to allocate to all the other categories; and what goals to pursue. But assuming you're more analytical—financial opposites often attract—it's okay for you to take the lead in crunching the numbers while you put your sanguine spouse in charge of brainstorming your next vacation. If you're *both* sanguines, use the least analytic budgeting tool of all: the envelope system.

If a sanguine has a job that's heavily dependent on commissions (which is often the case, since sanguines do well at sales), this can pose two challenges. First, a variable income mixed with a lack of interest in budgeting can lead to overspending. Second, a sanguine's optimism can make them assume the income they've generated in an unusually good month will continue every month. It's far better to budget for income conservatively, basing the number on an average of the past twelve months. In good months, bank the extra to cover a shortfall in a not-so-good month.

To stem a sanguine's tendency toward impulsive spending, set up some rules. For example, whenever you are faced with a potential purchase costing one hundred dollars or more, even if it's in the budget, first talk it over with your spouse, and then take another day to think about it some more.

If sanguine is your primary temperament type, here are some suggested verses of Scripture for you to reflect on and memorize.

- For encouragement in your generous ways: "You will be enriched in every way to be generous in every way, which through us will produce thanksgiving to God" (2 Corinthians 9:11).

- For remembering to slow down a bit and be careful about impulsive spending: "Desire without knowledge is not good, and whoever makes haste with his feet misses his way" (Proverbs 19:2).

- While it's fine to buy the latest fashions (as long as you can afford them!), for remembering not to take your identity from such things: "They exchanged the truth of God for a lie, and worshiped and served something created instead of the Creator, who is praised forever. Amen" (Romans 1:25, HCSB).

Choleric

If you're time sensitive, your primary temperament type may be *choleric*. That's my secondary type, and time management is one situation where it makes its presence felt. Being on time is really important to me. I get tense and irritable when I'm running late.

Cholerics are the type-A hard chargers. They're confident, goal oriented, practical (buy them gifts that are useful!), and self-sufficient. They prefer to work independently and thrive on pushing through obstacles to get things done. I have a good friend who is a very successful entrepreneur; he's a classic choleric. He's passionate, visionary, and highly driven.

Cholerics' time sensitivity and desire to move forward make them highly productive but also may lead them to make financial decisions without consulting their spouses. A choleric's tendency to take over household finances, paying the bills and making the investments, can leave their spouse ill prepared to handle household finances without them.[3] They can also be demanding of the person they're married to. Instead of taking an interest in what their spouse bought on a recent shopping trip, they're usually more interested in knowing how much they spent.

These get-stuff-done types have an especially strong work ethic. Ask them about their childhood, and they are likely to say they were earning money from an early age. One potential downside for this type may be a tendency toward workaholism.

Because they value results so much and are more task oriented than people oriented, cholerics need to be careful not to run people over as they go after their goals. In pursuing the absolute best price, I know there are times when I have pushed too hard. I still have to remind myself, *People first.*

If you have a choleric temperament, remember that when people look back on their lives, it isn't the business success they enjoyed or all they got done that will matter most; it's the people in their lives.

If choleric is your primary temperament type, here are some suggested verses for you to reflect on and memorize:

- For encouragement to use your leadership gifts as God directs: "Commit your work to the LORD, and your plans will be established" (Proverbs 16:3).

- For remembering that what you do isn't as important as how you do it, particularly how you treat people: "If I speak in the tongues of men or of angels, but do not have love, I am only a resounding gong or a clanging cymbal. If I have the gift of prophecy and can fathom all mysteries and all knowledge, and if I have a faith that can move mountains, but do not have love, I am nothing. If I give all I possess to the poor and give over my body to hardship that I may boast, but do not have love, I gain nothing" (1 Corinthians 13:1-3, NIV).

Jerry and Ramona Tuma, authors of *Smart Money*, an excellent book about the financial tendencies associated with each temperament type, point out that those words come from the Bible's classic choleric, the apostle Paul, who "knew from personal experience that love is the most important characteristic for a choleric to acquire."[4]

- To help ward off the tendency to place your confidence in your investments rather than in the Lord: "Whoever trusts in his riches will fall, but the righteous will flourish like a green leaf" (Proverbs 11:28).

Melancholy

There's a very strange type of person walking the earth: someone who actually *likes* to use a budget. Can you imagine? This unusual bird's primary temperament is *melancholy*. (*I* can imagine this because melancholy is my primary temperament type.)

People with a melancholy temperament tend to be introverted, dependable, and conscientious to the point of perfectionism. They can get a bit obsessive about details, insisting that their budget balance to the penny. Melancholies usually make good purchasing decisions because they thoroughly research them.

Last year, when we shopped for an SUV to replace a sixteen-year-old minivan, I filled in a detailed spreadsheet, comparing several vehicles across at least fifteen characteristics. We wanted a midsize SUV that had a legitimate third row, so I compared every third-row metric available: headroom, hip space, shoulder room. We ended up happy with our purchase (a Kia Telluride), but it took a while to make the decision, and I drove everyone a little crazy with the process, maybe myself most of all. While planning is a good thing, you do eventually need to take action, and melancholies don't move quickly.

Melancholies are thorough, persistent, good at anticipating problems (unlike cholerics, who tend to barrel ahead), and they like to have a plan. Once their plan is in place, they don't like to change course. On road trips, my far more spontaneous wife will see a billboard for what looks like a fun place to visit and suggest that we take the exit. I'll want to stick with the plan. Maybe I should start planning for five-hour trips to take six hours, building in room for side trips. Jude would get to be spontaneous, and for me, it would all be part of the plan!

As with each temperament, melancholies have seemingly contradictory sides. While they're usually good at controlling spending, they can overspend on things that speak to their strong aesthetic sense, such as beautiful clothing, artwork, gourmet food, books, or music. This might mean buying clothing less often so that when you do buy clothing, you can afford more expensive items.

According to Jerry and Ramona Tuma, no other temperament battles fear as intensely as the melancholy.[5] This can manifest itself in a tendency to worry and can even lead to depression. Financially, fear can lead melancholies to play it overly safe with their investments, and low self-esteem can hinder their careers because melancholies may underestimate themselves.

If melancholy is your primary temperament type, here are some suggested verses for you to reflect on and memorize:

- For encouragement about your desire to plan: "The plans of the diligent lead surely to abundance, but everyone who is hasty comes only to poverty" (Proverbs 21:5).

- For help overcoming fear: "God has not given us a spirit of fear, but of power and of love and of a sound mind" (2 Timothy 1:7, NKJV).

- If you're dealing with self-doubt: "I can do all things through him who strengthens me" (Philippians 4:13).

Phlegmatic

Have you been at the same company, or in the same type of position at different companies, for a long time? Do other people call you frugal, maybe even a little tight? Are you a saver of money and stuff? *Phlegmatic* may be your primary temperament type.

With their diplomatic, easygoing nature and their dry sense of humor, phlegmatics have been described as "the most likable of all the temperaments."[6]

Phlegmatics prefer to be in the stands than on the field. While they don't seek leadership positions, they can be very good, if reluctant, leaders. If a phlegmatic ends up in such a role, they won't be the bold, take-charge type of leader that a choleric would. They will move more slowly and be more supportive of their team.

Their cautious nature may cause phlegmatics to stay with certain jobs longer than they should and to invest very conservatively. If you're a phlegmatic, you may benefit from working with an investment advisor, who will drive decisions.

Frugal to a fault, and especially reluctant to spend money on themselves, phlegmatics may wear clothing long after it has worn out or gone out of style. As the wife of one phlegmatic said, "You can see how pained he becomes when you watch him give a tip. As he pulls it out of his wallet, he will massage the money with his fingers. He says he does this to make sure there are no bills stuck together, but I think he is saying goodbye to his money."[7] This is where a good plan can help. If you're a phlegmatic, commit ahead of time that whenever you go out to eat, you will give at least a 15-percent tip, preferably 20 percent. In the moment, it may still be tough to give that much, but making a commitment in advance should help.

While their stinginess can make generosity a challenge, when a phlegmatic learns to fully trust in God's provision, no one will be a more faithful giver, nor more consistent.

While phlegmatics don't like to shop, they are especially good bargain shoppers. It is impossible for a phlegmatic to pay full price for anything. They're also good researchers and planners, but they can have trouble pulling the trigger on a decision. While they don't like to negotiate, the Tumas point out that "you can never out-wait a phlegmatic,"[8] which can be an effective negotiation technique unto itself.

If phlegmatic is your primary temperament type, here are some suggested verses for you to reflect on and memorize:

- For encouragement in your tendency to be gracious toward others, whether members of your own family or your work team: "Be humble and gentle. Be patient with each other, making allowance for each other's faults because of your love" (Ephesians 4:2, TLB).

- For motivation toward greater generosity: "But since you excel in everything–in faith, in speech, in knowledge, in complete earnestness and in the love we have kindled in you—see that you also excel in this grace of giving" (2 Corinthians 8:7, NIV).

- For inspiration to move from planning, researching, and thinking about it to taking action: "If you wait for perfect conditions, you will never get anything done" (Ecclesiastes 11:4, TLB).

Know Thyself

That's a brief look at the four temperaments—sanguine, choleric, melancholy, and phlegmatic.[9]

As I said, temperament may be the most underrated factor that influences our views and uses of money. If you don't understand your temperament, you may end up living at the effect of it, often wondering why you do what you do with money and why you seem to keep bumping up against the same financial problems and conflicts again and again.

On the other hand, if you *do* understand your temperament, you have a great opportunity to maximize your inherent money-management strengths and work around your weaknesses.

Helping Our Kids Understand Their Temperaments

This isn't a topic to teach our kids about while they're toddlers. Although we may start to see in our children certain tendencies associated with specific temperaments at an early age, it's important to give them time and watch how they respond to a variety of situations.

Jonathan showed an early desire for order, lining up his toys just so, perhaps hinting at a primary temperament of phlegmatic, but it was too early to know for sure. When he entered the sixth grade, the many changes that came with moving to a new school with a very different routine led to a lot of frustration, unhappiness, and some anger. I saw elements of what could be a choleric or melancholy temperament.

Soon enough, he found his rhythm. As he enters his senior year of high school, the anger and moodiness are distant memories. What has emerged is an even-keeled yet driven and remarkably hardworking young man. He spends each morning and evening in God's Word, exercises six days a week, and works—whether on his homework or a school club he founded—in an impressively disciplined manner. Also, despite a challenging academic load, he is endlessly gracious and patient with people and quick to assume the best of them. When he went through the lists of characteristics, he scored highest for choleric (that's his driven, goal-oriented side) with a secondary temperament probably of phlegmatic (that's his quiet, diplomatic side, and also where he gets his hilarious dry wit).

Build on Strengths, Manage Weaknesses

As early as age twelve or thirteen, have your child go through the lists of characteristics associated with each temperament, check each one they think describes them, and then see which temperaments have the highest number of check marks. Separately, do the same thing yourself, checking each characteristic you think describes your child, and then compare results. (You can print copies of the checklist from mattaboutmoney.com/resources.) If you don't come to the same conclusion, that's okay. It can take time and exposure to a variety of life experiences to gain more clarity about their tendencies. Either way, it can be good to revisit this exercise a year or two down the road.

As their temperaments become clearer, talk with your children about what temperament-based strengths you see in them. Which ones do they see? How could those strengths be used in ministry or at school? How might they impact how they use money? Especially in their mid- to late teenage years, talk about how their temperaments could help point them toward what to study in college and what types of careers to pursue.

Sanguines will thrive in relational jobs where they are teaching, selling, making presentations, and/or working in teams. Their upbeat outlook also makes them well suited for caring professions. Cholerics will excel in leadership roles, perhaps in business, politics, sports, ministry, or the military. Melancholies will be good at jobs that require precision, self-sacrifice, and creativity, which brings a wide range of possibilities into view—perhaps the arts, education, or medicine. Phlegmatics will do well at jobs that require patience, discipline, and routine, making great engineers, money managers, or accountants.

For the sake of brevity, I've been using phrases like "Phlegmatics don't like to shop" and "Melancholies are thorough," but especially as we introduce this topic to our kids, we need to be careful here. We would be wise to avoid labeling our kids and to make sure they don't label themselves. They're not *a* sanguine. *Their primary temperament type is sanguine.*

The work of Stanford psychologist Dr. Carol Dweck can help us guide our children in seeing some of the inherent downsides to their temperaments in a healthy way. She's well known for her work on the topic of mindset, drawing an important distinction between a fixed mindset and a growth mindset.

We want our kids to approach this topic not with a *fixed mindset*, where they see themselves as victims of their temperament, judge themselves because of the weaknesses that come with it, or see their tendencies as carved in stone.

Instead, we want them to bring a *growth mindset* to the table, viewing their temperament as a helpful insight into how God has intentionally, purposefully, and wonderfully designed them.

We want them to see that understanding the inherent strengths that come with their temperament can help them maximize those strengths. In the process, they can discover more about where and how they could have their greatest God-glorifying impact. And we want them to see any weaknesses that come with their temperament as opportunities to learn, grow, and seek God's help in managing those weaknesses.[10]

> *When people believe their basic qualities can be developed, failures may still hurt, but failures don't define them.*
>
> CAROL DWECK, *MINDSET*

Yes, impulsiveness may come with a sanguine temperament, worry may come with a melancholy temperament, a tasks-over-people perspective may come with a choleric temperament, and indecision may come with a phlegmatic temperament. However, God is bigger than all of that. He can help our kids manage these tendencies if they ask Him for greater self-control, more faith, a people-first perspective, and His clear direction.

A Nudge in the Right Direction

We can help our kids as well, suggesting ways to build on their strengths and manage their temperament-related weaknesses.

Tips for Teens with a Sanguine Primary Temperament Type

If your child is especially brand conscious, teach her how to look for sales on her favorite brands. Introduce her to thrift stores where well-known brands can often be found for a fraction of their original cost. Because sanguines can be impulsive, suggest that she avoid email marketing lists, which will subject her to constant "deals." Encourage her to remember this mantra: "A deal isn't a deal unless it's a discount on something I was going to buy anyway."

Tips for Teens with a Choleric Primary Temperament Type
Your child may be especially willing to negotiate, so encourage him to hone this skill through practice. A garage sale would be an easy place to start. See how much of a discount he's comfortable asking for, and then encourage him to ask for more. By the same token, make sure he's willing to walk away. In addition, since a choleric temperament can cause a person to focus on the task at hand, make sure he treats sellers with kindness and respect.

Tips for Teens with a Melancholy Primary Temperament Type
If your child readily takes to the use of a budget, help her build that skill early. Perhaps start her with the envelope system or a paper-and-pencil approach, but introduce her to an online tool as soon as she has her own checking account. As she learns about investing, encourage her not to check on her portfolio's performance too often. That's good advice for everyone, but especially for people with a melancholy temperament, because down days in the market may stoke their fears.

Tips for Teens with a Phlegmatic Primary Temperament Type
People with a phlegmatic primary temperament type usually don't like to spend time or money shopping. Frugality can be a good thing, so applaud your child's budget-conscious ways. However, frugality gone too far *isn't* such a good thing. Show a phlegmatic teen how he can minimize his shopping time and still keep his

clothing somewhat current by going on quarterly shopping trips at stores where he has had success quickly finding things he likes.

Conclusion

Understanding one's temperament is not a one-and-done sort of exercise. Encourage your children to continue learning more about how God has uniquely designed them. It's a fascinating journey of discovery that will play an important role in helping them manage money well—and much more.

Recap and Next Steps

All of us have certain tendencies, financial and otherwise, that can be traced to our temperaments. The concept of temperament explains why some people have a hard time saving money and others save too much, why some are comfortable taking risks with their investments and others prefer to play it safe, and why some people make financial decisions quickly while others need more time. Each temperament comes with some inherent money-management strengths and weaknesses. By identifying our primary and secondary temperaments, we can learn to play to our strengths while managing our weaknesses. Helping our kids identify theirs will contribute greatly to their ability to manage money well.

- As early as age twelve or thirteen, have your kids go through the list of characteristics associated with each temperament, and do the same on their behalf. If your conclusions differ, that's okay. Revisit the exercise in another year or two.

- Talk with your kids about ways they see their temperaments influencing how they think about and use money. What natural money-management strengths do they see that can be attributed to temperament? How could they build on those strengths?

- What natural money-management weaknesses do your kids see that could be attributed to temperament? How could they manage those weaknesses?

- Discuss how your kids' temperaments could help them decide what to study in college and what to do for a living.

- Encourage your kids to memorize Psalm 139:14: "I praise you, for I am fearfully and wonderfully made. Wonderful are your works; my soul knows it very well."

CHAPTER 11

BUILDING GOD-HONORING
FINANCIAL HABITS THAT LAST

Do not be conformed to this world, but be transformed
by the renewal of your mind, that by testing you may discern
what is the will of God, what is good and acceptable and perfect.

ROMANS 12:2

WHEN WE LIVED IN THE CHICAGO AREA, we bought our house
from a psychiatrist and his wife. He and I struck up a bit of a
friendship, and one morning over breakfast I asked him some
questions about how to help effect life change. I had become somewhat discouraged by my experience as a coach in our church's
stewardship ministry. Too often, I would meet with someone who
was seeking a way out of a difficult financial situation, give them
what I thought was good counsel, and then meet with them again
in a couple of weeks only to find that not much had changed. I
wasn't expecting miracles in two weeks, but I was hoping to see
some progress. And I had this nagging sense that in too many cases,
the changes that *were* happening in the lives of people who came
to the ministry for help either weren't long-lasting or weren't very
comprehensive.

I had become convinced that knowledge alone isn't enough to bring about behavior change. If it were that simple, we'd all be brilliant money managers. After all, there's no shortage of readily available financial knowledge. For any question someone has about money, answers—sometimes even credible answers—can be found online. And yet, there continues to be no shortage of people who struggle to get the money thing right.

Drafting a Blueprint

When I met with my new friend that morning, I was excited about sharing this new theory I had. I thought we should focus first on identity. The Bible says that our identity—who we believe we are in our hearts—influences our decisions: As we think in our hearts, so we are (see Proverbs 23:7, AMP), and from our hearts "flow the springs of life" (Proverbs 4:23). As Christ's followers, we are stewards of His resources, or wise builders. Only after people really understand their identity should we get more practical by teaching what the Bible says about debt ("The borrower is servant to the lender"; Proverbs 22:7, TLB) and saving ("The wise man saves for the future"; Proverbs 21:20, TLB) and all the rest, as well as how to *do* what it says in very practical ways (like deciding whether to pay off high-interest or low-balance debt first). Then we should walk with them for a while as they live all this out. I thought this step-by-step process—identity first, then knowledge, and then behavior—had the potential to be more effective in helping people make positive, comprehensive, lasting changes. In essence, I saw the process as heart first (identity, worldview, attitudes), then head (knowledge), and then hands (behavior).

My new friend took it all in very patiently and politely. He asked some clarifying questions.

Then he said I had it *partly* right.

The part that he said was on track was the important role of identity. What we do does indeed largely flow out of who we are.

In his book *Atomic Habits*, James Clear suggests *choosing* the identity of who we want to be as a way of bringing about a desired change. As an example, he compares the approaches used by two people trying to quit smoking:

> When offered a smoke, the first person says, "No thanks, I'm trying to quit." It sounds like a reasonable response, but this person still believes they are a smoker who is trying to be something else. They are hoping their behavior will change while carrying around the same beliefs.
>
> The second person declines by saying, "No thanks. I'm not a smoker." It's a small difference, but this statement signals a shift in identity. Smoking was part of their former life, not their current one. They no longer identify as someone who smokes.[1]

Clear goes so far as to say, "Identity change is the North Star of habit change."[2] As Christians seeking to manage money in a wise, God-honoring way, I'm tempted to say that our task is not really about *choosing* an identity; it's about understanding who God has made us to be and then living into that identity. In reality, though, it's both. As we discussed in an earlier chapter, each of us did, in fact, *become* someone new when we placed our faith in Christ: We became children of God. It's important to understand that this is who we are. Financially, we became stewards of God's resources— or, as I prefer to say, wise builders who seek to build our lives and make financial decisions based on the solid rock of God's Word, not the shifting sand of our consumer culture.

But as we've also discussed, there's some choosing to do as well. The relentless force of our consumer culture requires us to daily "put off" the old self and "put on" the new (see Ephesians 4:22-24).

The Heart of the Matter

The work of identity can be hard ground to till. It seems so vague and intangible. That's why an article promising "Supermarket Super-Saver Shopping Secrets" is guaranteed to get far more engagement than a post about cultivating the heart of a steward. I get that. We're busy. We want answers. Picking up a quick tip or two that could save us some money seems like time well spent. Exploring matters of the heart seems like it could be a long slog toward an unknown destination.

And this is exactly why teaching our kids about money has so much promise. Their slates are as clean as they will ever be. There will never be a more opportune time to fill their hearts with God's Word and wisdom—to occupy that space before our consumer culture gets in there; to teach them and show them from their earliest days how to manage money according to God's principles and for His purposes. Doing this now means that they won't have to spend years undoing what Jude calls "stinkin' thinkin'" (believing the lies of the culture or of the evil one) and bad habits later. Doing this now means getting the fullest possible measure of exponential returns from orienting their use of money around loving God, loving people, and making a difference. What an incredible opportunity they have! And what an incredible opportunity *we* have to help point them in the right direction!

The Habit Circle

Here's the part my psychiatrist friend said was not quite right: He said that life change is not linear. It isn't that we first get the whole identity thing figured out and then move on to gaining the knowledge needed to live it out and then put that knowledge into practice. That's just not how things work in the real world. Life is far too messy.

All three components of life change or habit formation—identity, knowledge, and behavior—are important. But the process of utilizing them to live the lives we were intended to live isn't linear. It's circular. And there isn't a correct starting point. Nor do we always have to move around the circle in the same direction. And neither do the elements have to stay in the same order. Each one can and does reinforce and build off the others.

The key point is that all three are important. Heart transformation alone isn't enough to tell us what to do. Knowledge alone isn't enough to keep good behaviors going. And good behaviors alone are not enough to inspire new expressions of a growing faith. We need all three working in concert with each other.

Making Change

We adults—depending on where we are with our faith, financial knowledge, and money-management habits—may have some changes to make, and it may take some time to get to a better place. When I became a Christian at age twenty-nine, I had *a lot* of changes to make. One part of my life, which had nothing to do with money, seemed to change overnight. I used to swear very easily and very casually. Suddenly, I lost all desire to talk that way. I think that was the work of the Holy Spirit, cleansing me from the inside out. It was a very quick, very noticeable change. On the other hand, my financial situation did *not* change overnight. I still had twenty thousand dollars of credit-card debt, and there were times when it was deeply discouraging. The road ahead looked like it was going to stretch on forever. Then one night, in my first-ever Bible study, we read 2 Corinthians 12:7-10:

> So to keep me from becoming conceited because of the surpassing greatness of the revelations, a thorn was given me in the flesh, a messenger of Satan to harass me, to keep me from becoming conceited. Three times I pleaded with the Lord about this, that it should leave me. But he said to me, "My grace is sufficient for you, for my power is made perfect in weakness." Therefore I will boast all the more gladly of my weaknesses, so that the power of Christ may rest upon me. For the sake of Christ, then, I am content with weaknesses, insults, hardships, persecutions, and calamities. For when I am weak, then I am strong.

Those words spoke to me. They *ministered* to me. My debt felt like the nastiest of thorns that had been twisted into my flesh. Three times? I'd pleaded for relief many more times than that! But when I read, "My grace is sufficient for you, for my power is made perfect in weakness," it was as if a weight was lifted from my shoulders.

My debt wasn't going to just disappear, but those words helped me see a greater purpose for it. God had already used it to draw me into a relationship with Him. Now He was using it to keep me humble, to keep me leaning into Him for strength and encouragement, and to keep me growing in my relationship with Jesus.

I needed all three elements working together: heart transformation, knowledge, and action. Taking some practical steps to start getting out of debt was helpful, but it wasn't enough to keep me going. I needed to be bathed in God's Word. I needed time with the Lord in prayer. Reading Jesus' words in John 10:10, that He came that we might have life "abundantly," alongside Paul's words in 1 Corinthians 7:23, that I had been "bought with a price" (meaning my salvation had been secured through Jesus' sacrifice on the cross) so I should not become a slave to men (which is what I had become through my reckless use of money), reinforced the wisdom of living debt free. That strengthened my resolve, and every time I sent a big check to my creditors, it led me back into God's Word to learn more about His intentions for how I should live.

The more I read the Bible and the more time I spent with the Lord in prayer, the more I was filled with gratitude for all that He'd done and was continuing to do for me. My heart was being transformed. I was gaining more knowledge, both about God's Word generally and about what it teaches about money. And I was taking action. All three were working in concert—not always in the same order, but always building on each other.

It took me five years to pay off that twenty thousand dollars of credit-card debt and another year to pay off my car. Looking back, I can see how God used that time to shape my character and draw me closer to Him.

A Virtuous Cycle

One of my great hopes for this book is that our kids—yours and mine—won't have to learn financial lessons the hard way. My encouragement to you is to be sure to incorporate all three elements of habit formation into your teaching with your kids.

The easy part of this is teaching our kids what to do. But

making sure their habits stick requires getting their hearts involved. So as your kids help you sort laundry, teach them how to do the job well. But also, as you see the godly character traits of diligence and a good attitude emerge, be sure to affirm them. It's important to tie behavior and character together. And some nights when you put your kids to bed, read verses to them that relate to the financial lessons you're teaching (like 1 Corinthians 10:31, showing them that whatever they do, even sorting laundry, they can and should do for the glory of God).

As you move your kids along from saving a portion of every dollar they receive to saving for more expensive purchases, affirm their patience along the way. Read Proverbs 21:20 with them: "The wise man saves for the future, but the foolish man spends whatever he gets" (TLB). But also help them see God's heart behind such good and practical counsel. God loves them, and His Word is full of guidance given out of His love. He wants them to live free from the burden of financial stress.

Scripture memorization can play an important role in our children's development because, as Richard Foster notes, God uses such disciplines to shape our character: "They put us where [God] can work within us and transform us."[3] Having Scripture written on their hearts will help our kids differentiate between the many lies of our consumer culture and the truth of God's Word, guide their decisions, and empower them to live the lives God designed for them.[4]

Over time, keep opening the funnel. As your kids prove themselves able to be trusted with a little, trust them with more. Remember, the goal here is for them to leave our homes equipped and empowered to make good decisions on their own. We want their hearts full of God's Word so that it is the dominant influence over what they think and do. We want their heads full of the knowledge they need to make good, God-honoring decisions. And we want their hands full of strength, conditioned by plenty of practical, real-world experience.

> *There are probably few greater satisfactions to a parent than hearing that his child did a good thing with no one looking over her shoulder.*
>
> DR. HENRY CLOUD AND DR. JOHN TOWNSEND, *RAISING GREAT KIDS*

The longer our kids follow this path (walking with God, studying and meditating on His Word, and spending time with Him in prayer), grow in the knowledge of how to live out God's Word financially, and make daily decisions in accordance with God's principles and for His purposes, the more natural it will be for them to live as wise builders. I love the vision cast in Galatians 2:20: "I have been crucified with Christ. It is no longer I who live, but Christ who lives in me. And the life I now live in the flesh I live by faith in the Son of God, who loved me and gave himself for me."

May each of our kids be able to say the same one day.

The Most Important Money Lesson of All

As we discussed in chapter 6, the Marshmallow Test demonstrated the remarkable benefits that come to those who can delay gratification. Children who at age four demonstrated the ability to put off an immediate reward and wait for a better one were found later in life to be more resilient, better able to maintain friendships, and healthier than those who didn't.

Financially, the ability to delay gratification helps people save for cars instead of financing them, invest for future needs instead of becoming dependent on Social Security or family, and wait for items to go on sale instead of paying full price.

But it's so much more than that. The ability to delay gratification is the single most important character trait for living with the healthiest, most satisfying, most God-glorifying relationship with money. Let me explain.

Just Passing Through

Shortly after moving from Chicago to Louisville in 2012, I was in Chicago for a short visit. It was so good to be back in the city I love so much. I love the family and friends we have there. I love the city's lakefront, architecture, history, character, grittiness, diversity, and so much more.

On the last day of my visit, still drinking in my surroundings, I was shocked into reality by the sudden realization that I don't live there anymore. It's no longer my home. In an instant, my mood shifted from a deep sense of joy to a profound sense of sadness and loss.

But as I drove out of town, I sensed God telling me, "I have good plans for you and your family in Louisville." And I sensed him reminding me that whether I live in Chicago or Louisville or Timbuktu, *this* is not my home. According to the Bible, "our citizenship is in heaven" (Philippians 3:20).

Within that truth is the power to completely transform—to radically *improve*—our relationship with money. And if we can convey this truth to our kids, it will be the most important lesson they ever learn about money.

Looks Are Deceiving

So often, when someone has a ton of debt and a financial situation that just doesn't work, the common assumption is they need to cut back, tighten the belt, rein themselves in. But in many such cases, the real answer is far less intuitive. It isn't that they need to stop stretching themselves so far; it's that they need to stop settling for so little.

When we believe that this world is all there is, and when we fall for the lie that our self-worth and satisfaction depend on the brands we wear and drive, it's no wonder so many people so readily take on so much debt. Life is short. If this is our one and only shot at happiness, we'd better get all we can as soon as we can. The apostle Paul said that this misguided mindset can lead to a cavalier attitude: "Let us eat and drink, for tomorrow we die" (1 Corinthians 15:32).

A Little Taste of Heaven

Of course, Paul knew that this is *not* all there is. And he said that the Holy Spirit helps all believers experience that truth in very profound ways:

> For we know that the whole creation has been groaning together in the pains of childbirth until now. And not only the creation, but we ourselves, who have the firstfruits of the Spirit, groan inwardly as we wait eagerly for adoption as sons, the redemption of our bodies. For in this hope we were saved. Now hope that is seen is not hope. For who hopes for what he sees? But if we hope for what we do not see, we wait for it with patience. (Romans 8:22-25)

Incredibly, this—having "the firstfruits of the Spirit"—means that the Holy Spirit's presence within us gives us the ability to experience little tastes of heaven here and now. According to Paul, this naturally leads to two responses: a yearning for *all* of heaven, and also the patience to wait.

Is This as Good as It Gets?

So let me ask you: Do you long for heaven?

I have heard people say that they do. Honestly, though, when I first thought about it, I couldn't say that I did. At least, I didn't think so. Oh, I believe heaven is real. I'm just not in any hurry to get there!

If it seems that you don't yearn for heaven either, consider this: Maybe you do, and maybe I do too.

Think about some of the most powerful, deeply enjoyable experiences you've ever had—maybe an incredible vacation in a beautiful setting with your favorite people. You didn't want it to end, and your memory of it fills you with a longing for more.

C. S. Lewis said that in our enjoyment of such things there is something more going on than meets the eye:

> It was not *in* them, it only came *through* them, and what
> came through them was longing. . . . For they are not the
> thing itself; they are only the scent of a flower we have
> not found, the echo of a tune we have not heard, news
> from a country we have never yet visited.[5]

Mistaking them for *the thing itself* is where we go wrong. When we mistake the things or experiences money can buy for "the thing itself," we can easily find ourselves running on an exhausting and chronically disappointing treadmill of wanting, buying, and enjoying . . . and then quickly wanting again.

"If I find in myself a desire which no experience in this world can satisfy," Lewis said, "the most probable explanation is that I was made for another world."[6]

A Patient Yearning

The realization that even the greatest things of this world will never completely satisfy us is not bad news; it's *helpful* news. It takes the pressure off, freeing us to enjoy them for what they are—wonderful gifts from our generous and loving God, and even glimpses of a far greater joy yet to come, but not the basis of our identity or self-worth, and not the source of our greatest joy.

This perspective is the foundation of a healthy, satisfying, God-honoring relationship with money and what it can buy. I love how John Eldredge sums up the yearning Paul spoke of: We express our longing for God best when we "have the patience to enjoy what there is now to enjoy, while waiting with eager anticipation for the feast to come."[7]

Hope

When Focus on the Family asked if I'd like to write a book about family money management, I was so amazed at God's goodness, so grateful for the opportunity, and so ready with an idea. I knew that if I ever wrote another book, it would be this one. I've been involved in stewardship ministry long enough to have seen some wonderful examples of life change. At the same time, it bothers me to see far too many people struggling with the same issues I saw people dealing with when I first got involved in this work. Too many couples are fighting about money. Too many people are living in financial fear, just one missed paycheck away from disaster. Too many people are enslaved to debt. And too many people are living on the unsatisfying treadmill of want-and-buy-and-want-and-buy.

My prayer is that our kids—yours and mine—will grow up to be men and women who do the whole money thing differently. I hope they walk all their days in close, vibrant relationship with Jesus, taking their identity from their relationship with Him, not from anything they can buy. I hope they take great joy in living generously, regularly partnering with God by investing financially in His life-changing, eternity-shaping work. I hope they experience the sense of freedom that comes from having money in reserve and margin in their monthly budgets. I hope that money is never a source of stress or strife in their marriages but a tool that enriches their most valued relationships. I hope they get to experience the joy of having children of their own and that they pass these lessons along to them, and their children pass them on to their children, and on and on (see Deuteronomy 7:9). I hope that through their use of money, they draw ever closer to Jesus, love well the people He has placed in their lives, and use their talents, passions, and opportunities to make the God-glorifying difference they were uniquely designed to make.

I hope our kids always hold money and what it can buy with open hands, deeply enjoying what there is now to enjoy, and as they do, smiling with gratitude—so amazed at God's goodness, so thankful for each glimpse He gives them of the far greater joy that is yet to come.

Acknowledgments

My name might be on the cover, but there are many other people who have made this book possible.

To Warren Beach, who taught the first biblical money-management workshops I ever attended: Thank you for teaching God's Word on money with such clarity and humility. You sparked a passion that continues to this day.

To Ron Blue, Randy Alcorn, Howard Dayton, Chuck Bentley, and the late Larry Burkett: Your books have been instrumental in helping me build a biblical worldview about money.

To Dave Briggs and Tom Vislisel: Thank you for your friendship and all the wisdom you've poured into my life over the years, financial and otherwise.

To Austin Pryor and Mark Biller: Thank you for inviting me to be part of the Sound Mind Investing team. It's a privilege and honor to work for an organization that is intent on glorifying God and helping people with what is arguably the most difficult aspect of managing money. You have contributed mightily to my own growth as a steward of God's resources and in particular to my understanding of investing.

To Keith and Cag Wilson, who led the first parenting workshop Jude and I ever attended: The wisdom you imparted then, and many times since, continues to shape our lives in countless good ways.

To Larry Weeden, Vance Fry, and Kelly Kimbro at Focus on the Family: Larry, I will never forget the day I received your email and the conversation we had shortly thereafter. I don't know how God put me on your radar screen, but I'm so glad He did. Thank you for opening the door to such an unexpected and wonderful opportunity, and for what a pleasure it is to work with you. Vance, your expert guidance on the manuscript—always seasoned with much-needed grace and good humor—have made this a far better book than it would have been otherwise. And Kelly, thank you for patiently guiding me through the countless details involved in this journey.

To Robin Bermel and Sarah Susan Richardson at Tyndale House: Robin, what a happy surprise to cross paths with you again! Thank you for your wise and steady leadership over all things related to getting this book into the hands of as many people as can benefit from it. Sarah, thank you for so perfectly capturing the essence of the book.

To Erik Wolgemuth: One of the greatest days of my life was the day you, Robert, and Andrew agreed to work with me. It's an honor to partner with you again. I'm so grateful for your wise counsel and friendship.

To the many people who generously shared your experiences in teaching your kids about money and allowing me to tell your stories in this book: I only wish I had heard your ideas earlier so that Jude and I could have incorporated them into our parenting sooner!

To the many friends who have prayed me through this book-writing journey, including the Man Challenge guys who gather far too early on Thursday mornings—Jeremy, Chris H., Chris B., Matt F., Matt O., Cody, Andrew, Rob, and Mitch: Our conversations have grown me as a Christ follower, a husband, and a dad. And it's just a lot of fun to hang out with you, despite the hour.

To our Tuesday evening small group: Chuck and Alison, George and Julie, James and Amanda, Steve and Angie, Neil and Andrea, and Grant and Anne. It's a gift to be able to study God's Word with you, to enjoy your friendship, and to have been on the receiving end of your many prayers related to this book and so much else.

To the women who get together with Jude most Thursday mornings to pray: Alison, Jen, Mindy, Dominique, and Karen. What you do is so countercultural, sacrificial, and effective! And also to Jude's dear friends Susan and Sheila. Thank you all for bathing our family and this book journey in prayer. It has made a huge difference.

To my longtime friend and primary mentor, Dick Towner: You have taught me countless lessons about managing money from a biblical perspective, but you've done so much more than that. By the example of your remarkably generous, grace-filled, others-centered life, you have shown me what it looks like to be a Christian man. And what a blessing that when someone gets the pleasure of knowing Dick Towner, Sibyl comes with the package! Dick and Sibyl, your influence runs deep in our marriage and our parenting. Jude and I are so grateful.

To Wayne Riendeau: Thank you for your boldness in speaking Truth into my life at just the right time. That changed everything. Of course, this book wouldn't exist otherwise.

To Mark Salavitch, John Fuhler, and Joe Ruh: Your friendship means more to me than I could ever express. Our conversations, adventures, laughter, and tears have added a richness to my life that is beyond measure. So much of what I have done since meeting you, including writing this book, has been wonderfully shaped by the time we have spent together.

To Jonathan, Andrew, and Annika: I could never put into words what a joy it is to be your dad. You amaze me and inspire me. You make me laugh, and you move me to tears. May God grant you short memories of my many parenting mistakes and a deep, unshakable understanding of how much your mom and I love you. God has already done so much in you and through you, and He's just getting started!

And mostly, to Jude: When I first saw you, I wanted to meet you. And when I met you, I only wanted to spend more time with you. It's been the honor of my life to have now spent twenty-three years traveling this crazy up and down journey together as husband and wife. The wisdom, beauty, and joy you have brought into my life are immeasurable. Of course, all the ideas in this book have been cultivated together with you. Because of you, I look back with a heart full of gratitude, and I look forward with eager anticipation. To borrow some words from Robert Browning: "Grow old along with me! The best is yet to be . . ."

Notes

INTRODUCTION | MORE THAN MONEY

1. Dr. Henry Cloud and Dr. John Townsend, *Raising Great Kids* (Grand Rapids, MI: Zondervan, 1999), 106–7.

CHAPTER 1 | ENDLESS POTENTIAL

1. Jim Collins, *Good to Great* (New York: HarperCollins, 2001), 164.
2. Collins, *Good to Great*, 164–65.

CHAPTER 2 | GROWING UP AS A TARGET MARKET

1. Jenny Radesky, Yolanda Reid Chassiakos, Nusheen Ameenuddin, and Dipesh Navsaria, "Digital Advertising to Children," *Pediatrics*, July 2020, https://pediatrics.aappublications.org/content/146/1/e20201681.
2. Radesky et al., "Digital Advertising to Children."
3. Susan Strasser, *Satisfaction Guaranteed* (Washington: Smithsonian Institution Press, 1989), 27.
4. Juliet Schor, *The Overworked American*, (New York: Basic Books, 1991), 119.
5. William Leach, *Land of Desire* (New York: Pantheon Books, 1993), 149.
6. Radesky et al., "Digital Advertising to Children."
7. Kim Bhasin, "A 5-Year-Old Girl Gives Her Verdict on Famous Logos, and Some Fail Miserably," *Business Insider*, January 31, 2012, https://www.businessinsider.com/these-brand-logos-get-put-to-the-test-by-a-5-year-old-girl-and-some-fail-miserably-2012-1.

8. Jeanna Bryner, "Even a 3-Year-Old Understands the Power of Advertising," *Live Science*, March 9, 2010, https://www.livescience.com/6181-3-year -understands-power-advertising.html.

9. Pamela Steensland, "Piper Sandler Completes 42nd Semi-Annual Generation Z Survey of 10,000 U.S. Teens," Piper Sandler, October 5, 2021, https://bit.ly/2YFJZal.

10. *The Social Dilemma*, directed by Jeff Orlowski (Boulder, CO: Exposure Labs, 2020).

11. Amy Crouch and Andy Crouch, *My Tech-Wise Life* (Grand Rapids, MI: Baker Books, 2020), 47–48.

12. American Academy of Pediatrics, "American Academy of Pediatrics Announces New Recommendations for Children's Media Use," NewsWise, October 21, 2016, https://www.newswise.com/articles/american-academy -of-pediatrics-announces-new-recommendations-for-children-s-media-use.

13. *The Social Dilemma*.

14. Andy Crouch, *The Tech-Wise Family* (Grand Rapids, MI: Baker Books, 2017), 68–69.

15. Sebastian DeGrazia, *Of Time, Work and Leisure* (New York: Vintage Books, 1990), 225.

CHAPTER 3 | LEARNING TO EARN

1. Dorothy Sayers, *Why Work?* (Monee, IL: CreateSpace, 2014), 20.

2. Martin Luther King Jr., "What is Your Life's Blueprint?," Beacon Press, May 19, 2015, https://www.youtube.com/watch?v=ZmtOGXreTOU.

3. Angela Duckworth, *Grit* (New York: Simon & Schuster, 2016), 212–13.

4. Duckworth, *Grit*, 219.

5. Dr. Henry Cloud and Dr. John Townsend, *Boundaries with Kids* (Grand Rapids, MI: Zondervan, 1998), 140.

6. Cloud and Townsend, *Boundaries with Kids*, 136–37.

7. Sheila Seifert, "Age-Appropriate Chores for Kids," Focus on the Family, https://www.focusonthefamily.com/uncategorized/age-appropriate-chores -for-kids. Also see this guide: "I Did It All by Myself! An Age-by-Age Guide to Teaching Your Child Life Skills," https://www.familyeducation .com/life/individuality/i-did-it-all-myself-age-age-guide-teaching-your -child-life-skills.

8. Julie Lythcott-Haims, *How to Raise an Adult* (New York: Henry Holt and Company, 2015), 197–98.

9. Duckworth, *Grit*, 225.

10. Duckworth, *Grit*, 88.

11. "How Much Will I Earn in My Lifetime?," CalcXML, https://www.calcxml
.com/do/ins07.

CHAPTER 4 | PLANNING TO SUCCEED

1. Jeffrey Dew, "Bank on It: Thrifty Couples Are the Happiest,"
http://www.stateofourunions.org/2009/bank_on_it.php.

CHAPTER 5 | LIVING GENEROUSLY

1. Elizabeth Dunn and Michael Norton, *Happy Money* (New York: Simon
& Schuster, 2013), 109–10.
2. Does your family enjoy music? Listening to certain songs with our kids
and singing along can also be a powerful way to reinforce these lessons
of gratitude. To dwell on God's goodness toward us, I highly recommend
Michael Olson's "Everything Is a Gift" (*Sacred Invitation*, 2010).

CHAPTER 6 | SAVING PATIENTLY

1. Martha Deevy, Jialu Liu Streeter, Andrea Hasler, and Annamaria Lusardi,
"Financial Resilience in America," Stanford Center on Longevity and
Global Financial Literacy Excellence Center, August 2021, https://
gflec.org/wp-content/uploads/2021/08/Financial-Resilience-in-America
-Report-August-2021.pdf?x53868.
2. Walter Mischel, *The Marshmallow Test* (New York: Little, Brown and
Company, 2014), 23–24.
3. Mischel, *The Marshmallow Test*, 24–25, 167.
4. Mischel, *The Marshmallow Test*, 95.
5. Mischel, *The Marshmallow Test*, 28.
6. Nikki Cox, "Let's Think of Future Us," *No Sidebar* (blog),
https://nosidebar.com/lets-think-of-future-us.
7. Cox, "Let's Think of Future Us."
8. Mischel, *The Marshmallow Test*, 72.
9. Mischel, *The Marshmallow Test*, 101.

CHAPTER 7 | MULTIPLYING MONEY

1. IRA eligibility depends on your income and whether you're covered by a
workplace retirement plan. The latest rules and regulations are available
at mattaboutmoney.com.
2. Dimensional Fund Advisors data from Daryl Bahls, "90 Years of
Performance: Strategic Planning for Investing at Every Stage of Life,"
Paul Merriman, https://paulmerriman.com/90-years-of-evidence-shows
-investor-patience-leads-to-better-returns.

3. There's a third, even more aggressive option that I describe at mattaboutmoney.com. It requires more involvement but has produced even better results.

4. If money is withdrawn from a Roth to help pay for college, that will be treated as income and will be factored into the financial aid formulas.

CHAPTER 8 | SPENDING SMART

1. For more on health care sharing ministries, read Joseph Slife, "Health Care Sharing Ministries: A Christian Alternative to Health Insurance," Sound Mind Investing, https://bit.ly/3mUStDf.

2. Mary Hunt, *Raising Financially Confident Kids* (Grand Rapids, MI: Revell, 2012), 33–36.

CHAPTER 9 | BORROWING CAUTIOUSLY

1. Jeffrey Dew, "Bank on It: Thrifty Couples Are the Happiest," http://www.stateofourunions.org/2009/bank_on_it.php.

2. To compare the two methods with your debts—paying off highest-interest-rate debts vs. lowest-balance debts first—use the calculator found at https://unbury.me.

3. This example assumes an 18-percent interest rate and a minimum payment of 2 percent of the balance or a minimum of fifteen dollars. Try some other examples using this calculator: https://www.bankrate.com/calculators/credit-cards/credit-card-minimum-payment.aspx./.

4. To understand all the factors that impact your credit score, go to https://www.myfico.com/credit-education/whats-in-your-credit-score.

5. There are some unique implications of authorized-user credit-card purchases in terms of how those purchases will show up in your online budget program and how your kids will need to track these purchases. For details on how to handle all this, go to mattaboutmoney.com and search "authorized user."

6. There's an example of such an agreement at mattaboutmoney.com.

7. One of many student-loan calculators freely available on the internet is this one: https://www.bankrate.com/loans/student-loans/student-loan-calculator.

8. Estimates of starting salaries can be found at the US Bureau of Labor Statistics' Occupational Outlook Handbook (https://www.bls.gov/ooh) or salary.com (https://www.salary.com).

CHAPTER 10 | OUR INNER MONEY MANAGER

1. Tim LaHaye, *Spirit-Controlled Temperament* (La Mesa, CA: Post, Inc., 1992), v.

2. LaHaye, *Spirit-Controlled Temperament*, 16.
3. A Bible study I highly recommend is "Set Your House in Order," which will help you organize your finances so that your spouse would be prepared to handle the household finances if something were to happen to you. It's available from the financial discipleship ministry Compass - finances God's way at https://compass1.org.
4. Jerry and Ramona Tuma, *Smart Money* (Sisters, OR: Multnomah Books, 1994), 61.
5. Tuma, *Smart Money*, 70.
6. Tuma, *Smart Money*, 80.
7. Tuma, *Smart Money*, 86–87.
8. Tuma, *Smart Money*, 85.
9. For more insights into each temperament's tendencies and a look at how particular temperament combinations tend to play out, I highly recommend Jerry and Ramona Tuma's book *Smart Money*.
10. Carol Dweck, *Mindset* (Great Britain: Robinson, 2017), 6, 13.

CHAPTER 11 | BUILDING GOD-HONORING FINANCIAL HABITS THAT LAST
1. James Clear, *Atomic Habits* (New York: Avery, 2018), 32.
2. Clear, *Atomic Habits*, 40.
3. Richard Foster, *Celebration of Discipline* (New York: HarperCollins, 1988), 7.
4. At mattaboutmoney.com is a document with a more comprehensive list of verses of Scripture that relate to various financial topics.
5. C. S. Lewis, *The Weight of Glory* (New York: Touchstone, 1980), 29.
6. C. S. Lewis, *Mere Christianity* (New York: Touchstone, 1980), 121.
7. Brent Curtis and John Eldredge, *The Sacred Romance* (Nashville: Thomas Nelson, 1997), 199.